HOW
to keep your
FOCUS

Sunday Adelaja

How to keep your focus

Sunday Adelaja

Paperback

Copyright © Golden Pen Limited
Milton Keynes, United Kingdom. All rights reserved
www.goldenpenpublishing.com

Quotations of the Scriptures are taken
from the New King James version of the Bible.

Why do people with great potential in life miss their chance to be successful? Why do they fail to realize their abilities and talents and fulfill their calling? What hinders these people from walking in God's plan and carrying out the great work that only they are able to complete? In this book you will find the answers to these questions and many others.

This book or parts thereof may not be reproduced in any form, stored in a retrieval system, or transmitted in any form by any means — electronic, mechanical, photocopy, recording, or otherwise — without prior written permission of the author.

All rights reserved

Copyright © 2016 Sunday Adelaja

ISBN: 978-1-908040-49-7
ISBN-13: 978-1908040497

How to keep your focus. — Milton Keynes, UK: Golden Pen Limited, 2016 — 139 p.

CONTENTS

Chapter 1. Live is given only once 4
- Life is an opportunity
- Seek first the Kingdom of God...
- Well done! Good and faithful servant!

Chapter 2. What is important to know about success? 12
- I have a dream...
- What is real success?
- How do you find your calling?
- Reaching success by taking God's paths
- The purpose of success and prosperity
- Success does not just happen
- Failure is the womb of success

Chapter 3. Reasons for every failure.. 37
- Excuses, excuses
- Do not judge and you will not be judged
- Do not be deceived
- Forget the past

Chapter 4. How to use opportunities 49
- Much food is found in the fallow ground of the poor
- For who has despised the day of small things?
- Whoever is greatest among you should become the least
- Faithful in a little is faithful in much

Chapter 5. How to manage yourself 58
- God resists the proud
- The great power of self-discipline and self-management
- The pain of self-discipline
- A person with self-control is better than a person who takes a city

Chapter 6. Let your 'yes' be a 'yes' 71
- Be perfect as your Heavenly Father is perfect
- ...All liars shall have their part in the lake which burns with fire and brimstone...
- Not My will but Your will be done

Chapter 7. The power of a decision 80
- You alone decide where you will be tomorrow
- Having made a decision, begin to act
- How to complete a task

Chapter 8. Be unwavering 95
- Do not throw away your confidence
- Save your soul your patience
- Not by might and not by power
- You need to fight for success
- Run to receive

Chapter 9. Quenching the arrows of the evil one 106
- Those who endure to the end will be saved
- What are these pitiful Jews doing?
- The fervent prayer of a righteous man avails much

- ...And we set a watch against them
- It is reported among the nations
- I am doing a great work

Chapter 10. The ability to organize your business or ministry 121

- One man cannot win the battle
- The importance of sound administration
- The purpose that unites
- Accountability and control
- The harvest is ripe but the laborers are few
- Money answers all things

AUTHOR'S FOREWORD

We have probably all at one time in our life, set before ourselves a goal. However, sometimes many of us have become distracted, and therefore have not reached our goal. That is why we cannot underestimate the role of focus in our lives. It is because of a lack of focus that the dreams of our childhood and youth fade away. Many of us have already forgotten what we used to dream about. Focus gives a person unlimited possibilities. What exactly is focus? You can find many definitions for this word in the dictionary. I will refer to those definitions that apply to the context of this book. A famous Russian dictionary written by Vladimir Daal gives the meaning of FOCUS as the distance ahead of us that the eye can see clearly and well. Sergey Ozhegov gives an interesting definition of the word: "FOCUS is the point at which the optical instrument creates a distinct picture of an object; also FOCUS is concentration or the center". If a person can keep his focus then he is concentrated and purposeful. He is a person of zeal and power. He is a person who knows his goal, purpose, and destiny. This is because focus opens all doors and helps him to achieve the very best results.

I hope this advice about how to become focused in life will make you a focused person. I pray that you will learn to turn away from seemingly good, attractive ideas that distract you from your calling, so you can receive the very best. I also believe this book will help you to be focused not on things of secondary importance but of primary importance, so you will clearly know what to refuse and what to keep and when to say "yes" or "no" in life. This can become a decisive factor in your life and destiny. Read this book and may it guide you to complete the goals and tasks that have been placed before you. May God bless you.

INTRODUCTION

God has made every person special, unique, and different. Everybody can do something that no one else can do. Unfortunately, only a few people have the ability to fulfill everything that the Lord has called them to do.

I get so sad when I see the people who could lead this world and be a source of encouragement and support for others totally sidetracked and in need of help themselves. Why does this happen? Why do people with great potential in life miss their chance of becoming successful and fulfilling their calling? What hinders them from carrying out a great work that only they are capable of doing?

One of the main reasons, to explain this, is the inability to define life goals and be focused on them. This is true not only in one sphere of life but in every sphere of life, whether this is in business, family, education or relationships with friends, etc. This is very important because at times the devil tries to divert all of our attention in only one direction, forcing us to forget that life is not just one-sided. This is the reason why often successful businessmen do not have happy personal lives. In order to avoid similar situations, we have to learn how to keep all of our priorities as the main focus in our lives. This will help us to reach our goals and fulfill our purpose, or in other words to have a life that is successful and happy. To be able to keep focused requires great effort. What does it mean? As I have already written, to begin with, this means being single minded and not wavering like a leaf blown by the wind or a wave tossed to and fro by the sea. To keep focused also means to be passionate and zealous toward the goals that have been placed before you. Without this, you will achieve nothing in life.

To be focused also means to concentrate on three levels. On the level of your spirit you are required to meditate and pray about your goals. The second level is that of your soul where you have to continually remember your goals and your tasks. The third is the physical level, which re-quires you to do everything you can in your own physical strength in order to attain your goal. Focus can be compared to dedication. A focused person is a dedicated person. It is a person who does not give up half way through or does something half-heartedly or allows his hands to slacken. He always gives one hundred percent.

It could also be said that the ability to keep your focus, is also having an intensive concentration. It is to give out all your inner strength. Of course, balance is necessary because if you are intensely focused all the time then you will quickly burn out and if you are fully relaxed all the time, you will get nothing done in life. Therefore in order to get results, there are times when you have to be very focused like a karate expert who can break bricks with one accurate blow of his hand. The secret of this phenomenon is not in the power of the blow but in the intense concentration that is released by tremendous energy, which allows this person to do what others cannot. If you had the same ability to keep focused on your life priorities then nothing would be impossible for you. Focus can open every door.

How can we learn to be focused and understand what we have been called to do? These are the things I want to talk about in the pages of this book.

CHAPTER 1

LIFE IS GIVEN ONLY ONCE

Before we try to work out what we are called to do and how we can keep our focus in order to be successful in life, it is necessary to know what life really is. Without this understanding our achievements will bring us neither happiness nor joy.

LIFE IS AN OPPORTUNITY

So what is life? I am concerned that most people only begin to think about this question toward the end of their lives, when there is no time to change or make a correction. Why does this happen? It is because for the most part we do not take life seriously. We think that it will last forever. We think that life belongs to us and so we arrange our lives in whatever way we want. However, this is a great deception. Wise people understand that life is a gift that has been given to us by God.

Life is God's trust to us.

Life is an investment to spend now on the earth so that later it will provide for us throughout eternity.

Life is also an opportunity. However, this opportunity is only given once. God wants us to use this chance so that later we will not be tormented by the thoughtless way that we wasted our years. That is why

Moses asked God to teach him and the nation of Israel how to number their days, (see Psalm 90:12) or how to fully use every day God had given them.

However, why is it necessary for us to take life so seriously? The reason is because life is not our own possession. One day we will have to give an account of how we spent our lives before the One Who made us and gave us this gift of life as a loan. The Bible says,

So then, each of us shall give an account of himself to God.

Romans 14:12

What do you think of this? If you are uncomfortable with this idea then it means that you feel you have left something undone or you have something lacking in your life. You have something you would be ashamed of if you were to stand before your Creator now. However, do not despair! While you are alive God is still giving you the chance to repent and make a correction to some things. However, you need to remember that one day there will be no more chances. One day there will be no church, no wife, and no children, or in other words, there will be no-one that you will be able to hide behind or point your finger at to blame for all your problems. There will just be you and God. He knows everything you do both in private and in the open. This means each one of us (we all stand naked before Him). Remember what is written in First Corinthians "...each one's work will become clear..." (1 Corinthians 3:13). At that time you will either be joyful if God praises you or terrified if He says,

'And cast the unprofitable servant into the outer darkness: there will be weeping and gnashing of teeth.'

Matthew 25:30.

SEEK FIRST THE KINGDOM OF GOD...

As I get older I have become more and more aware of the words of wise king Solomon when he said,

It is better to go to the house of mourning, than to go to the house of feasting: for that is the end of all men; and the living will lay it to his heart.

Ecclesiastes 7:2

Why did Solomon come to this conclusion? The fact of the matter is that tears and sadness cause us to think about life and make us separate the important from the not so important and the tares from the wheat. For me personally, it is always an opportunity to take a close look at my life and correctly organize my priorities in life. However, more importantly, whenever I have the chance to be in the "house of tears" I value it as a chance to redirect myself and my life so when I meet with the Lord, I will not be ashamed of anything. This is the most important thing in life. Many people do not experience happiness in their lives because they do not understand this truth. They are seeking satisfaction in their career, family, money, success, and achievements. All these things are not bad. Even God Himself does not want us to have need of anything. However, all of these things are of secondary importance.

The main focus and priority of any person should be his relationship with God and the fulfilment of His will. Jesus often openly talked about this:

Jesus said to them, "My food is to do the will of Him who sent Me, and to finish His work."

John 4:34

If our main motivation in life was to please God, then everything else would be without problems.

But seek first the kingdom of God and His righteousness, and all these things shall be added to you.

Matthew 6:33

This is a spiritual law that no-one can escape. So what is the Kingdom of God? It is "...not eating and drinking, but righteousness and peace and joy in the Holy Spirit" (Romans 14:17).

Most people are overly concerned and preoccupied by what they are going to eat and drink. They have forgotten to find life itself. If you do not find life then nothing will help you to experience true satisfaction, not even your work, family, fame, or wealth. Real life is found in Jesus Christ.

Jesus said to him, "I am the way, the truth, and the life. No one comes to the Father except through Me."

John 14:6

When you find life in Jesus Christ you will understand how wonderful it is to enjoy your family, money, and work. Otherwise if you spend all of your strength, energy and talents on the fulfillment of your own purposes and not on the fulfillment of God's purposes you will never become truly happy. This is very important to understand. I intend to give a lot of attention to this subject in this book because I want to talk about your calling. I will address how not to lose focus on the goals that are set before you. If you are sidetracked from your most important focus, which is The Lord, then this book will be simply useless. Unfortunately, very often when we attain some kind of goal we immediately forget about God. This is the biggest mistake we can make in life. Please remember your priorities: first of all find the true life which is in Christ and cling to Him with all your heart and try, as the apostle Paul teaches us, to think more about heavenly things and not earthly things (see Colossians 3:1,2).

These eternal values should be the main focus of our lives, "For what profit is it to a man if he gains the whole world, and is himself destroyed or lost?" (Luke 9:25). How awful is it to really gain the whole world and then lose it all? In the mass media we constantly hear about the deaths of prominent personalities of this world. The only thing that will remain in the memory of people about them is their good deeds, and what they did for others and the Kingdom of God.

One day Jesus appeared to a very famous preacher and said, "You do many good things on the earth however, you will only receive five percent for the work you have done as a reward in heaven." The preacher was very surprised, but Jesus explained to Him, "In heaven only those things that were done for the sake of the Kingdom of God and for the sake of God and His people are noted."

What does this mean? For example, if you had one million dollars and you spent only one hundred dollars for God's purposes, in your heavenly account, only those one hundred dollars would be recorded. However, if you had only one hundred dollars and out of this you spent ninety dollars for the purposes of God, in your heavenly account you would be a millionaire. Do you understand this? In heaven only those talents, resources, and energies that were spent for the sake of God and His Kingdom are noted. Everything else will simply be burnt up.

Many of us are not ready to meet with Jesus because we live our lives for ourselves and not for Jesus. However, I am personally ready to die right now; I am ready to go to heaven and I would not regret anything. This is because I value heaven more than the earth and I know the reason why I still live on the earth: it is for me to please heaven.

If this is the only thing that keeps a person on this earth then death, as the apostle Paul said, will be a gain. God wants us to learn to be ready to die at any moment without a single regret. For this, we need to live with a pure conscience before people and God every day and give ourselves totally to pleasing Him, serving people and fulfilling His will on the earth.

Well Done! Good and Faithful Servant!

My mind is focused on heaven and until the Lord takes me, I will work hard so that I will not fall. I know that one day I will meet with God face to face and He will say to me, "Sunday, you of course were far from perfect. You made many mistakes. Nevertheless, you tried, and even when you made a mistake, you always did everything to glorify Me. Therefore, well done!"

Everything I am writing here is of utmost significance and must be taken seriously. Do not treat this lightly; the devil does not want you to think about what will happen to you after death. "Why talk about this and why think about heaven?" — the devil says. However, I want to say to you that the hope to stand before God as a faithful servant both cleanses and strengthens us. I do not know what motivates your actions. For me this question has already been settled. Heaven dictates to me what my actions must be; and it is not negotiable. Again, I will only hear Him say,

"...Well done, good and faithful servant; you were faithful over a few things, I will make you ruler over many things. Enter into the joy of your lord."

Matthew 25:21

Who wants to enter into the joy of His Lord? Perhaps, each one of us would like to hear this praise from God. However, this does not happen automatically. This depends on how serious we treat life and how soberly we value the time that has been given to us on this earth, and whether we maximize our efforts to do all things. If God today has given us the chance to think about this, then it means He is giving us the chance to re-evaluate our lives and start living in the Godly way that would free us from being tormented for the years we have wasted.

GOLDEN TRUTHS

- Life is an opportunity.
- Each one of us will give an account before God.
- The purpose of life is to fulfill the will of God.
- Seek first the Kingdom of God and His righteousness and all these other things shall be added to you.

CHAPTER 2

WHAT IS IMPORTANT TO KNOW ABOUT SUCCESS?

We have understood what life is and why it was given to us. Now let us look at what a successful life really is.

I would not be mistaken if I say that everybody, without exception, desires to be successful. This is true. This is true for every person even if people pretend that they have no desire to succeed or prosper. However, in reality these people, just like the rest of us, really do not want to live in poverty. They also want to have enough money to look after their children and send them to a prestigious school, purchase a spacious apartment or house and a decent car and enjoy trips abroad. Believe me when I tell you that no- one wants to live a miserable life. It is the desire and dream of each and every one to be successful. Dreaming is not a bad thing. In fact, dreaming is good because a successful life begins with our dreams.

I HAVE A DREAM...

If a person does not have a dream then he lives an empty and useless life. He lives a life full of disappointments. This is because, for instance, if a man has no plans for his family then he is automatically planning for failure in this sphere of his life. If he is a businessman and he does not dream about the expansion of his business then he is also planning for its collapse.

This is true in any sphere of a person's life.

New ideas, dreams, and goals are natural for a person. This is the nature of God which He has placed in us. It is His image and likeness.

Why does God place dreams and desires in our hearts?

First of all they help us to see the possibilities and goals that we can aim for. They give us the opportunity to think about the future and reach for it. Also, it is God's method to help us understand that in the future, after our life on the earth, we can look forward to eternal life in the Lord Jesus Christ.

Secondly, when we have a dream we are motivated to fulfill it. We begin to release from within ourselves the gifts, talents, and potentials that the Lord has placed in each one of us. It also causes us to eventually become just as God planned for us to be from the beginning, or in other words to be successful. This is the best position for us.

So the ability to dream is an important and valuable human resource. Whoever you are and whatever terrible condition you may be suffering now, you have within you, all the possible gifts that could help you to succeed in life.

Therefore, dream and make plans, and most important of all, fulfill these plans in your life. We will talk about how to do this in the following chapters, but for now let us once again return to the question of what the definitions of success and a successful person are?

WHAT IS REAL SUCCESS?

The fact is that success is associated, first of all, with people who have material wealth. However, the truth is, success does not mean one must have riches and it is not based on material values. A person may have millions of dollars but at the same time may not be successful. In actual fact, you cannot call the majority of rich people successful. For example in

America, statistics reveal that most suicides are not committed by African Americans or by native Indians on the reservations but by the people in the circle of Hollywood millionaires. Nevertheless, we continue to admire their way of life. What is good about it? The image that is portrayed by the mass media does not show us the way things really are. If everything was so beautiful like we perceive from the movies and television then these "successful" people would never think about taking their own lives. If their family lives' were as happy as we read in the glossy magazines then they would not need to change their spouse so often.

The concept of happiness that has been formed by the world is just an illusion. "Acquire wealth, fame, popularity, and position in society and then you will be a successful person!" This is the so called "formula for success" but it is a fallacy that is leading this modern world to a dead end and pushing people into alcohol and drug addiction, prison, and suicide. It is not worth making the sacrifice for this kind of success.

Do you know what the people who use this formula to gain such success experience? Total disillusionment! The cruel reality is that after they have tried and invested all their energy and the best years of their lives in order to reach the peak of success, they find that behind all the riches, fame, and position in society, there is in actual fact nothing. It is all meaningless. Then, as a result of this hopeless state, all the orgies, drunkenness, and suicides begin. Why does this happen? As mentioned already, it is because success does not mean having material riches and a position in society. Success does not depend on how much money you have and it does not mean fame, and it is not an outer manifestation of what is in you. Yes, if a person is successful then in most cases he will have material riches. However, this is just the consequence of being successful. If a person is really successful then first of all he will have peace with God and with himself, and be in harmony with his family and the world around him.

This is only possible when a person finds his life calling and with God's principles, begins to fulfill his purpose and advance the Kingdom of God. That is the complete picture of real success.

HOW DO YOU FIND YOUR CALLING?

Before anything else, real success is to understand why you were created and to know what your calling is. It is the most important priority to be focused on. I have written more about this in many books such as "Fulfill your calling", "The road to greatness", "Victory despite the devil" and "Pastoring without tears." I have given this theme much attention because I understand that if a person does not know the reason why he was born, then his life is just meaningless. If you look on the outside it would seem that this person is living well, he is earning good money and holds a leadership position. However, if you look at his soul you will see that it is just ashes. This is because when purpose is not known abuse is inevitable and the worst thing is to abuse your own life. As you have already understood, all of us have only one life and if we do not know why it was given to us in time, then we will have a totally unavoidable disappointing life. This is why we need to literally focus all our attention in understanding what we have been called to do otherwise, why live if we do not know the purpose of our life? A really successful person knows he was not created as some people often joke: to simply give birth, get married, and then die. Our lives should not be empty and useless. We need to have a revelation from God concerning our lives because: "Where there is no revelation, the people cast off restraint; but happy is he who keeps the law" (Proverbs 29:18).

Most people live on this earth blindly because they have totally removed the question of God from their lives. They do not seek Him to receive His instructions and suggestions on their purpose and calling in life. Only God

Who formed us in our mother's womb and Who knew us before we were born can help us to know what our calling and purpose is in life. Therefore having been born, and having attained adulthood, we should turn to the Source of our life and ask the question, "Lord why did you create me and send me into this world?" God never creates and allows anything to come into this world accidentally or for no reason at all. If God has allowed someone to be born then that means He has a special purpose for this person. God has a unique purpose for each and every one of us and it is essential that we know this purpose. Otherwise, without a revelation from above a person has no goal and no focus.

What does this mean? Imagine a wild horse. How does it act? Of course, it acts unpredictably. You do not know what to expect at any given moment. God forbid that you should go near such a horse. The consequences could be disastrous because a wild horse is extremely dangerous. It is the same with people. A person who has no goal in life and does not have God's revelation and a clear understanding of why he is living on this earth, where he is going, and what his purpose is, is like a misguided missile. His life is like an endless experiment. He could do anything at any moment because he has no connection to the future or to a higher purpose that could act as a restraint. However, it is a completely different thing to meet a person who knows why he is alive and who has a word from God that leads him through his life like a guiding star. It is a pleasure to know such a person. He is peaceful and confident in himself and he always attains the goals that God has set before him. It is great to find such a person like this who knows what he wants and where he is going. The whole world will give way on the road for such a person as this. This has been proved by life itself. If a million people were walking along one road competing for first place but they did not know what they wanted in life then all their efforts would be in vain. However, if among them there was just one person who knew what he wanted and where he was going, then you would see that everyone else would give way to him on the road. A person who knows what he wants in life and where he is going is a bold, daring, and focused person. He is not afraid of the circumstances, difficulties, problems, and challenges that he meets along the path of life. Nehemiah, of whom I will make several references to in this book was a person like this. It is written in the book of Nehemiah:

Then I said to them, "You see the distress that we are in, how Jerusalem lies waste, and its gates are burned with fire. Come and let us build the wall of Jerusalem, that we may no longer be a reproach." And I told them of the hand of my God which had been good upon me, and also of the king's words that he had spoken to me.

So they said, "Let us rise up and build." Then they set their hands to this good work. But when Sanballat the Horonite, Tobiah the Ammonite official, and Geshem the Arab heard of it, they laughed at us and despised us, and said, "What is this thing that you are doing? Will you rebel against the king?" So I answered them, and said to them, "The God of heaven Himself will prosper us; therefore we His servants will arise and build, but you have no heritage or right or memorial in Jerusalem."

Nehemiah 2:17-20

Nehemiah faced one huge and what appeared to be a practically unsolvable problem in his life, which was the restoration of a city and, on an even larger scale, the restoration of an entire country. However, he gathered together a team and created an army and raised the spirit of his people, so that what he had thought of and planned could be fulfilled. Just think about how many problems stood in the path of Nehemiah. However, he overcame each one of these obstacles, only because he was focused on what both he and God wanted. Mountains will melt and rivers will dry up and become pathways, if you really know what you want and determine where you are going. In the example of Nehemiah we see that despite all the threats, attacks, and dangers in his life and the lives' of the people he led, decisiveness and the knowledge of what he wanted, defeated all the circumstances.

I want to say to you, that to be successful in life is absolutely no problem at all. A person only has to stand on the foundation of the Word of God and on God's faithfulness. So what exactly is the Word of God? It is the foundation of everything. The whole universe is held up by the Word of God. Imagine that! It is written, that if the Word of God comes into a person's life, he becomes a god. Remember the words of Jesus, "I and My Father are one" (John 10:30).

In other words, a revelation from the Word of God revealed from God, makes you a god over specific circumstances. Having received a word concerning healing, you become a god over your illness. When you receive a word about prosperity, you become the lord and god over poverty. This is the same in every sphere of our lives. For example, it is easy for me to be a pastor without tears because I have received a revelation from God about how to be a pastor without tears. When the Word of God also reveals to you about how to be, for example, a successful business-man then it will be an easy task for you to accomplish. You will know exactly how and what to do. Therefore, to be happy, successful, and rich is not a problem because when the light of the revelation of God's Word comes to you, you begin to shine. Through revelation from God's Word, you will rise up out of ashes, ruin, and chaos. If you are today on the brink of bankruptcy, you can still rise up again. All that is needed is for the light of the Word of God to shine through to you. When the light of the Gospel penetrates your life you will begin to shine forth. You will shine because of the light of God's revelation. This is why before we begin to move forward and before we rise up to success in life, it is essential that we lay up within ourselves a strong foundation of the Word of God. This is something that will keep us from falling.

Every person should have a certain lofty goal that is much bigger than himself and his own ability. It should be something that will live on after he has gone. As the black political activist and preacher Martin Luther King, who was against racial discrimination once said, "I submit to you that if a man hasn't discovered something he will die for, he isn't fit to live." If you have a task or a goal for which you are ready to give your own life then it means that you have something within you that will keep you from straying from the true path.

How do you get to know and understand what your calling is? There are whole seminars and many sermons that have been devoted to this theme. However, I will only make a few basic comments on this topic.

Apart from seeking the answer to this question from God Himself, you can get to know what you have been called to do, first of all by looking at yourself and your character. This is because when you were born, God put within you specific qualities that give you a hint on the direction and goal to head toward. Therefore get to know your own character and what your inclinations are. Having understood your character traits, you then need to find out where these qualities could be used and put them into practice.

Secondly, you need to search within yourself and find out about those things that evoke you to passion, what challenges you, what stirs inside of you both the feelings of hatred and love? What do I mean by this? If for example, having walked past a drug addict or an alcoholic the two emotions of love and hatred are stirred up within you at the same time: love for the alcoholics and hatred toward drug addiction or alcoholism, then those emotions are your indicators that God wants to solve this problem through you. It is God giving you the challenge to take up the responsibility for the fate of such people, and this is connected to your calling. Or for example, when people are talking about the church and about how the church does not have the influence it should have in society and you feel pain and zeal about this situation. It is in God's plan to use you so that the church would really become as victorious as the Lord has planned from the beginning. This is what the challenge of God is and the call of your purpose.

Thirdly, it is essential that you comprehend which sphere of activity you feel most at home in. That is where your place is and it is where you will be able to discover your calling. Nevertheless, please do not think a person only has one calling. God may have placed tens or even hundreds of callings within a person. However, it is important to define at least a few of them and immediately begin to work on them. Why is this important? This is because, it is only when you have found your main calling that you will then find the other ten or more callings in the land where milk and honey flow, in the land where everything in your life is taken care of. Remember in Exodus it is written:

The LORD God planted a garden eastward in Eden, and there He put the man whom He had formed. And out of the ground the LORD God made every tree grow that is pleasant to the sight and good for food. The tree of life was also in the midst of the garden, and the tree of the knowledge of good and evil. Now a river went out of Eden to water the garden, and from there it parted and became four riverheads. The name of the first is Pishon; it is the one which skirts the whole land of Havilah, where there is gold. And the gold of that land is good. Bdellium and the onyx stone are there. The name of the

second river is Gihon; it is the one which goes around the whole land of Cush. The name of the third river is Hiddekel; it is the one which goes toward the east of Assyria. The fourth river is the Euphrates. Then the LORD God took the man and put him in the garden of Eden to tend and keep it.

Genesis 2:8-15

What is this scripture talking about? It means that when we are busy working out our calling, we will always find out that God has already prepared for us before time, gold and precious things. In other words, He has provided us with everything we need for life. That is why it is so important to find your land, your purpose, and your place in life. Otherwise, there will be only problems, disappointments, complete torment, and no life.

However, finding your purpose in life is not everything.

REACHING SUCCESS BY TAKING GOD'S PATHS

Having found your calling, it is then very necessary to find God and know Him intimately, so that by taking His paths you will successfully fulfill your purpose. This is another area that we need to be focused on. What are God's paths? It is a righteous and holy life that is submitted to God's laws.

Unfortunately, many people who have discovered their calling in life begin to fulfill it but not by God's principles or paths. They go along the path of sin and lawlessness. However, this path always leads to the destruction of man both morally as well as physically. If God does not become your ideal and if you do not make the decision to live by his principles, then at some point in time you will find yourself shipwrecked. Goals achieved by not following God's paths are filled with sadness, sorrow, disappointments, fears, and broken hearts. What is the reason for all of this? It is because the person does not allow God's standards to discipline him and place him within the borders of true freedom. Only God's principles and not money or fame can make us

truly free. This is very important because only a free man can reign in life. However, if you are still living under the dictates of the flesh then you are not yet a king, you are still a slave. What exactly is the flesh? It is made from the dust. So if the earth is reigning over you, how then can you reign over it? In order to reign over the earth you have to be free from it, that is to say, free from the dictates of the flesh. The key to complete and true freedom is the Word of God or God's commandments. That is why when we come to the Lord at the beginning, He cuts all our worldly ways away from us and says to us, "seek first the Kingdom of God and His righteousness", this is because without the truths of the Kingdom of God and without His righteousness we cannot reign in life. Only truth establishes the throne of a king. Therefore, if there is no truth or righteousness in your life then do not be deceived, for regardless of how high you reach; you will still be a slave. This is why it is so important that before we move forward toward our goals we need to establish righteousness and holiness in every sphere of our lives. Then having become free spiritually, emotionally, and physically we can begin to reign. My book "Kings and Judges of the Earth" talks about this.

When we move toward our goals by choosing God's paths, this does not only keep us from destruction, it also makes our lives even richer because the path of God is safe, protected ,and insured; it is a blessing that brings no sorrow with it (See Proverbs 10-22).

When God blesses you there is no need to worry about your family because you know that they are under God's protection. When God has His hand of blessing on your life you do not have to be concerned about your business because you know that you are living by God's laws. You know you are acting in accordance with His Word that cleanses you, teaches you and helps you to avoid misfortune. It is a blessing that does not bring any sorrow, disappointment, and pain with it. Why? It is because you have already found the meaning and essence of life itself. Now you can enjoy all that God gives to you.

THE PURPOSE FOR HAVING SUCCESS AND PROSPERITY

However, even if you attain success by taking God's paths but you do not understand the purpose for this blessing or the fact that God gave you the fame, wealth, and position in society in order to establish His Kingdom on the earth, so that His will would be done on the earth as it is in heaven, then abuse is inevitable. An incorrect understanding of the purpose of having success will destroy you in the end because it will lead you where you do not need to go. It is like wanting to go to a city but taking a road that goes in the opposite direction. In order to arrive at the goal, the path should be precisely defined. For example, why is the ministry such a heavy burden for many pastors? It is because they did not understand the goals of their ministry. For instance, many people after the fall of the Soviet Union became pastors because it was fashion-able to do so, but they did not understand the most important thing, that is, that one should work in the ministry for one purpose only, which is to bring the Kingdom of God to the earth. Why do we see so many rich people wasting the money they have made in casinos, on prostitutes, or buy-ing drugs? The answer is the same. When the purpose is unknown then abuse is inevitable. Therefore it is not only necessary to find your calling and fulfill it with the help of God's principles but to use this calling in accordance with its purpose.

Why and for whom does God want us to shine and be successful and fulfilled? Why does God want us to be exalted? This is also another area that we need to pay attention to.

This then raises the questions, what are the purposes of prosperity and success?

First of all, God wants us to prosper not only for our own sake but also for the sake of others.

Now the LORD had said to Abram: "Get out of your country, from your family and from your father's house, to a land that I will show you. I will make you a great nation; I will bless you and make your name great; and you shall be a blessing."

Genesis 12:1,2

The phrase **"...and you will be a blessing"** talks about the fact that God wants to raise each one of us up so we would become a source of blessing to others. We need to see ourselves this way. You are a blessing to your relatives, friends, colleagues, and all people. This blessing is not just for you. If you are working just for yourself then you will never have peace because the fear of losing your wealth will paralyze your heart. I am talking here about prosperity that brings with it peace and tranquility. If you want to have this in your life then you have to become a blessing for all people. This also includes becoming a blessing to the poor because the Bible says,

Whoever shuts his ears to the cry of the poor will also cry himself and not be heard.

Proverbs 21:13

It is a terrible thing when God shuts His ears to us. Then nothing can help you, not even money or fame. Therefore, when God gives you prosperity it is very important not to lose the feeling of compassion so that you do not fall away from God's purpose for your life. When you see a person in need, help him. That is one reason why God wants to bless us.

Secondly, God gives blessing and prosperity in order to lift up His church.

Now it shall come to pass in the latter days that the mountain of the LORD's house shall be established on the top of the mountains, and shall be exalted above the hills; and all nations shall flow to it.

Isaiah 2:2

The Mountain of the Lord is the church. God's purpose is to make the church the cornerstone and lift it up in society. When God begins to bless you with finances and position in society do not forget that He gives you all of this so you can advance God's projects, and lift up the authority of the church in society.

Thirdly, God will bless His people in order to show the world that it is more profitable to live uprightly.

The righteous shall flourish like a palm tree, he shall grow like a cedar in Lebanon. Those who are planted in the house of the LORD shall flourish in the courts of our God. They shall still bear fruit in old age; they shall be fresh and flourishing, to declare that the LORD is upright; He is my rock, and there is no unrighteousness in Him.

Psalm 92:12-15

At the same time as blessing the righteous with wealth, position in society, health, and long life, God will also teach a lesson to those who ignore His principles in their lives.

Apart from this, God will bless the righteous "...to declare that the

LORD is upright; He is my rock, and there is no unrighteousness in Him" (Psalm 92:15). God really wants people to know His righteousness.

Why does God give His children prosperity? It is written in the Scriptures:

> **"Then you say in your heart, 'My power and the might of my hand have gained me this wealth.' "And you shall remember the LORD your God, for it is He who gives you power to get wealth, that He may establish His covenant which He swore to your fathers, as it is this day."**
>
> **Deuteronomy 8:17,18**

People who do not know God tend to think that they alone were responsible for all their achievements. However, God blesses people not so that they can become proud, but so that they can glorify the One Who gave them the grace and power to become successful and wealthy. Why does God not want us to become proud of ourselves and boast about our own achievements? The world considers this to be normal. However, God really loves us. He knows that pride comes before the fall. Every person that lifts himself up in pride is prophesying his own destruction, and this will sooner or later come to pass without any doubt. If we forget or ignore this truth from God we could lose all of our achievements in one moment. Therefore God guides our focus in the right direction. Nobody can have anything in this earth unless it was first given to him from heaven. It is God Who gives us the power to do everything. It is God Who opens the necessary doors at the right time. It is God Who makes us talented and gives us abilities. For all of these things we must give glory to God!

Another thing that God wants is that His people would expand His Kingdom through prosperity.

Again proclaim, saying, 'Thus says the LORD of hosts: "My cities shall again spread out through prosperity; The LORD will again comfort Zion, and will again choose Jerusalem."

Zechariah 1:17

Imagine if we did not have any money, we would not be able to rent a building in order to gather together and worship God. If we did not have any finances we would not be able to publish evangelical newspapers and Christian television programs through which many people have repented and have begun to go to church. We could not open rehabilitation centers for drug addicts and alcoholics. Thanks to all these things we are able to expand the Kingdom of God. Until the Gospel is preached to the ends of the earth, the second coming of Jesus Christ will not happen. Therefore for this reason, God wants to give prosperity to His people so that God would be able to spread the Good News throughout the earth.

God also gives prosperity to the righteous because He desires for them to have real joy in Him.

Let them shout for joy and be glad, Who favor my righteous cause; and let them say continually, "Let the LORD be magnified, Who has pleasure in the prosperity of His servant."

Psalm 35:27

God is the true source of joy. Therefore God's children do not need to look for artificial ways of getting satisfaction. Those who do not know the purpose of their success and prosperity will spend all their money seeking all possible forms of entertainment and will lose everything; their family, wealth, reputation, and health. To avoid falling into this same trap, we should understand and remember that true joy can only be found in the

Lord. The devil does not slumber and is ready at any moment to give you something counterfeit. As it is a foregone conclusion that inherent in prosperity there are many temptations, some believers think that it is better to live in need. They do not want God to bless them financially. However, whether we want this or not God cannot but give us financial blessing because He has already sworn by Himself, to give prosperity to His people. Prosperity is God's covenant with us. Here is yet another reason why God wants to bless us with success; it is to fulfill His covenant to us. He is a faithful God and He cannot reject His own word.

"And you shall remember the LORD your God, for it is He who gives you power to get wealth, that He may establish His covenant which He swore to your fathers, as it is this day."

Deuteronomy 8:18

God Himself made this decision. He became poor that we might be rich because of this covenant.

For you know the grace of our Lord Jesus Christ, that though He was rich, yet for your sakes He became poor, that you through His poverty might become rich.

2 Corinthians 8:9

In the same way as by the stripes of Jesus Christ we are healed, so too He took our sins so that every believer in Him can by faith enter into God's provision. This is also a covenant. There is no need for you to think that a 200-dol- lar salary is enough. God Himself willingly became poor so that we could become rich. You could of course erase this scripture from the Bible but that fact would still remain. Earlier we mentioned that everything we have has been given to us by God. Why then can riches and prosperity not be from Him. I will repeat again, prosperity is God's covenant.

My covenant I will not break, nor alter the word that has gone out of My lips.

Psalm 89:34

Regardless of how you oppose riches, God will never break His covenant. If you are serving Him and you are living by His laws then He will fulfill His promise to you even without your agreement. The problem is not the prosperity. Money by itself is not evil. Money is only paper and a means of attaining specific goals. The idea of money being good or evil does not exist. That same money can bring with it either good or evil. It all depends on who has the money. Money in the hands of a criminal will bring evil, but money in the hands of the righteous will always bring good. So the question is not about money but about people and how clean their hearts are. If your heart is filled with evil then you will use your money for evil but if you have a good heart then this money will help you to do good; by using it to bless other people. This is the real heart of the matter. Finally, think about this: if money comes from God then can it really carry within itself something bad? Of course not. God does not warn us to avoid prosperity. He warns us not to have a love for money. This has no relationship to prosperity itself. Did you know that even the poorest and most down trodden person can have a love for money? Do you think that he is a good person? Watch what will happen when he gets hold of some money. Therefore you need to fight in your own heart against the love of money. It is the root of all evil. You do not need to fight against prosperity. God gives us prosperity so we can build His church, develop the economy of the country, bring believers into a place of power and influence and help those in need. So how do we fight against the love of money? For this, God has set up the laws of tithing and sowing. Some people, especially non-believers, ask the question, why does God need our money? Of course God really has no need of our money. These laws were put in place not for His sake but for our sake. He did this so that we, having learned to freely part with money, might truly become free people and masters of money which will enable God to trust us with millions.

SUCCESS DOES NOT JUST HAPPEN

One other thing that we need to know about success is that it never happens by accident. A person becomes successful because he is prepared to become the answer to the needs of other people. Your determination to help people is a stairway to success and the more people you help, the quicker you will reach the peak of success. That is why Jesus said,

"...If anyone desires to be first, he shall be last of all and servant of all."

Mark 9:35

Serve people and solve their problems and then you will not even realize that you have become a successful and respected person. This is the law of life. Sitting on the sofa and meditating on yourself and your problems will never cause you to become successful. Here is one more very im-portant thing to mention. A person that works for the sake of money and a salary will also never become successful. This person is just thinking about his survival. Surviving is not life at all it is only existence. A successful person gives life to other people and gives it to them in abundance. Real successful people do not work for salary. Real successful people work in order to develop themselves; the gifts and the talents the Lord has placed within them. Most people cannot become successful because they are waiting for a better job or a higher salary. This is their problem and the root of their incompetence in life. However, all you have to do is selflessly solve the problems of the company where you work, and offer your services and then serve with all your heart. I am telling you that money will find its way to you sooner or a later as a result. This is a principle of the Kingdom of God. Do not seek your own needs but the needs of others. Serve people with what you have and soon you will see how God will raise you up and provide for you.

FAILURE IS THE WOMB OF SUCCESS

One more piece of wisdom you need to know about success is the fact that all success begins from failure. Always keep your focus on this law of life. But why does this happen? Why is failure inevitable? This is because the prince of this world, the devil hates success, especially the success of a believer. Why? Because it is written in the Bible, that the devil comes only to steal, kill and destroy (see John 10:10). If the devil is given a place, he will always steal success, prosperity, and wealth. This is his assignment.

Knowing this, the person who becomes successful is the one who, first of all, is not afraid of failure. The fear of failure is one of the main reasons why people fall to their knees before the circumstances and challenges in life. Due to the fear of failure many people who were naturally gifted to be millionaires, leaders of countries, and outstanding personalities do not do anything to be successful in life. These people have already failed. The fear of failure is worse than failure itself. The fear of death is worse than death itself. The fear itself is worse than the reality of what you fear. Therefore, if you want to be successful then the first thing you have to do is fight against the fear of failure.

I also want to add that the fear of failure is real. It is right to believe that failure will pay you a visit one day, but it is to make you successful later.

Secondly, you need to remember that any failure is just another step toward success. This is the law of the Universe. Look at the greatest failure in the history of mankind, the Son of God came to this earth and they took Him and murdered Him. This was the most humiliating defeat but it was followed by the greatest victory in the history of mankind.

Therefore any misfortune that comes along your path is a signal that victory is waiting for you. So if you have suffered defeat in some area then glory to God, you are on the right path. One set of American statistic says that one in ten new businesses collapse within the first year. What do these statistics prove? If you have less than ten defeats then you still have another chance to be successful and therefore you have no reason to be disappointed. Successful businessmen have between five to ten businesses going on at the same time so that even if nine of them fail, there will be one that will cover the other nine failures. Besides the fact that this business will compensate for the other nine, the most important thing is that these nine business failures will become the foundation for the one successful business. If there had not been those other nine failures then the necessary skills to create one large and successful venture would never have been acquired.

Thirdly, it is essential for us to understand that every failure teaches us how not to do something, it shows the wrong approach to attain our goal. This is good because at times we think we already know everything. Do you know why? This is because when we think we know something then we will act according to our thought. However, in practice just because you know something in your mind does not guarantee that you will avoid failure. Only when this knowledge has become a part of you and an integral part of your being, can you hope for success. Therefore to be successful, at times it is necessary to make the same mistake more than once.

Fourthly, you need to know that a successful person never gives up. Whoever does not surrender will not suffer defeat and he who surrenders has already lost. Winners never give up. Winners can lose but they will never give up! This is a principle: "For a righteous man may fall seven times and rise again..." (Proverbs 24:16).

If you want to be successful then you should never refuse to start something again from the beginning. I want to give you an example from one of my books "Who are you in history": "Winners never give up. The foundation of victory is confidence in the fact that you are in the center of God's will. If you have ascertained that your dream is from God and you have received confirmation that what you are doing is God's will then you should never give up irrespective of what the circumstances are, even if you are not successful the first, second, or even tenth time. Temporary loss does not mean total defeat. Failure does not mean that is the end. Failure is only a failure for people who think like that. Let each failure be for each one of us a stimulus to find other ways to achieve our goals. This kind of attitude toward life defines who the winners in this life are." We all of course know who Abraham Lincoln was. However, how many of you know the thorny path that he took before he became The President of the United States of America? In 1832 he lost his job and was defeated in the run for Illinois State Legislature; in 1833 he had a business failure; in 1836 he had a nervous breakdown. In 1838 he was defeated in the run for Illinois House Speaker. In 1843 he was defeated in the run for nomination for U.S Congress. In 1848 he lost the re-nomination. In 1854 he was defeated in the run for U.S Senate. In 1856 he was defeated in the run for nomination for Vice President; in 1858 he was again defeated in the run for U.S Senate. Nevertheless, in 1860 he finally became The President of the United States of America and one of the best American presidents of all time. What does this story tell us? It tells us that every failure only increases the probability of success. That is, of course, if the person does not give up and quit.

Fifthly, failure and defeat are not the most terrible things that can happen in life. The most terrible thing is to do nothing in life and to never complete the things you have started. It is worse to give up without a fight, to doubt everything and risk nothing. Without risk it is impossible to achieve anything of significance in life. I remember when I had just become a preacher, I could not even last half a day without food, but at the same time I knew there was great power in fasting and praying. Therefore, one day I made the decision to go away for a two day fast without food or water. I was terrified because I thought I might die. However, I took the risk and did not die. In addition to that, God rewarded me when He manifested His miracles through me during a church service after the fast. At that time I came to a very important conclusion; God can use anybody even the simplest person if only that person would take a risk, pay the price, and show diligence in his calling. With all these things in place that person would not die but he would live to see great success in his life.

Success, respect, and recognition in life do not come to you because you get older, as many people think. These things come only as a result of your readiness to take a risk and assume responsibility for your life. Honor and respect come regardless of age, into the lives of those people who have dared to do something. For example, who are the people who become millionaires? It is not the most intelligent but it is those who take the risk of stepping out of the boat and taking responsibility and launching out ahead, not fearing if they stumble or fall. Those who are afraid to take a risk will spend the rest of their lives working for only salary and criticizing their employers and the government. They will be slaves right up until the very end of their days;

Sixthly, it is important to know that before God can trust a person with success He has to first trust him with failure. These are very serious issues.

Any successful person will tell you how painful and unpleasant it is to pass through failures. It is difficult when you lose everything you have and when you feel like the most foolish person in the world, when everybody is laughing at you. It is really not easy to go through it. However, I want to say, that the people who have suffered defeat can hold their heads higher than those who never do anything and who have never experienced a terrible failure. However, this is possible only if the person after defeat does not quit but keeps moving forward. Otherwise, automatically he will go down to the same level as a real loser in life. God will only grant success to those that can be trusted with defeat and failure. Failure could be called the womb of success because every success was born out of some failure.

Seventhly, you should not live with the memory of your failures. They need to be left in the past. Many people do not begin anything new because they continually dwell on the memories of their past mistakes. However, if you are always thinking about your past mistakes, it is similar to carrying around a dead corpse on your back wherever you go. However, this will not last very long. The poisonous corpse will begin to kill you. What must we do then? Just as in school, we must work on our mistakes and draw out of these failures the appropriate lessons and then leave the past behind and begin to do something new.

GOLDEN TRUTHS

• The ability to dream is the most important human resource given to man by God.

• Without a dream, life is meaningless.

• Real success is not defined by materialistic values.

• Real success is to understand why you were made and to know what your calling is. — Only God can correctly tell another person what his true purpose in life is.

• You will only find everything necessary for a happy and successful life in the Promised Land of your calling.

• Only God's principles and not fame and money can make a person truly free.

• The willingness to become the answer to the needs of other people is what makes a person really successful.

• Every success begins with some kind of a failure.

CHAPTER 3

REASONS FOR EVERY FAILURE

We have already mentioned to a certain extent in the first chapter, what a person must do in order to be successful, and at the same time what can hinder a person from achieving success. First of all, it is a person's unwillingness to inquire of God His divine purpose for his life and seek to understand Him. It is also the neglect to honor God's commandments, and also the fear of failure or the wrong perception of it. What are the other reasons for lack of success?

EXCUSES, EXCUSES...

Probably you have heard others said, or you yourself have used the following phrases, "Things are not working out for me in my life because my parents did not teach me how to live, because the economy collapsed, because my spouse left me, because I have no money..." and similar other sayings. Do you know what all of this is called? Making excuses and finding justifications.

The overwhelming majority of people on this earth do not become successful because they have achieved the status of a specialist in making excuses and explaining why they cannot do one thing or the other. Instead, it is these self-justifications and excuses that make them failures. These kinds of people constantly complain that everything around them is wrong. They say the country they live in is not the right one, the government is not good, and their neighbors and boss are bad. This is the same all over the world. Many people are trying to migrate to America be-cause they think that everything in America is perfect. However, even in this "paradise" there are lots of frustrated people. What does this prove? This proves that the reason for the lack of success of any person, be it an Ukrainian, a Chinese or an American is not because of external factors but the inner life of the person; his worldview, conscience, and perception of life.

The people who are living in defeat have a mind that is dead. The reason for their lack of success can be explained by the fact that they believe they will never achieve anything. In reality, this is exactly what happens because how a person thinks, so he is. In other words, success or defeat in life depends on how you think. If you believe you will succeed then you will, and if you do not you will not, the choice is yours.

Do you remember the story of David and Goliath in the first book of Kings, the seventeenth chapter? What do you think? Logically, who should have been stronger, a king with his full armor or a seventeen year old shepherd boy? Which of these two had greater possibilities? Of course, judging from the physical point of view, a king with his appearance and army could do much more than one teenager. However, which of them killed Goliath? It was the young lad who simply believed he had the power to deal with the problem coming from the giant from the opposing army.

What does this story teach us? What truth does it carry within itself? It is teaching us that instead of finding ten thousand excuses why something cannot be done, it is better to find one reason why it can be done. Clearly, this is not easy. Excuses and justifications lie on the surface and they come to us from every direction as soon as we set our minds to do something with our lives. However, in the midst of all of these comments, "it is impossible, it cannot be done, there is no way..." all that is needed is to find only one reason why it is possible and why it can be done. Find, cling to, and focus on an argument (reason) why you can succeed in life and why you do not have to be held back by your family or society. Instead, believe that you can be a blessing not only to your relatives and those closest to you but also to the whole world. Right now think of and write down five or ten of your desires which are, according to your point of view, unrealistic and impossible and then write alongside them at least one reason why nevertheless, it could still be done. If you are a believer then this task is much easier. You have a very great reason why you should succeed in life. It is because of the fact that there is nothing impossible to the believer because the God Who created the heaven and the earth lives in you. He is the God Who holds the whole universe in the palm of his hand. He is the God Who crushed the might of Egypt and led a whole nation through the Red Sea. He is the God Who died for you on the cross and was raised back to life on the third day to deliver you from hell and give you eternal life. If you believe in the Living God and serve Him with all your heart and all your might, and you do everything that you have to do then, He will do everything that He can, which no man can do. You would therefore not be dependent on social welfare from the government, or on the opinions of your employers, or relatives that say you are not good for anything. Their opinions would not affect you because you would only believe God's opinion which says,

I can do all things through Christ who strengthens me.

Philippians 4:13

Therefore, "I cannot", "it is impossible", "it cannot be done", and "I do not know" are all expressions of failures. If you want to be like this then continue to live and use these expressions! However, God is saying something different, "All things are possible to the believer". You can do all things through Christ Who strengthens you. Always keep focused on this revelation from God.

DO NOT JUDGE AND YOU WILL NOT BE JUDGED

We have just seen that the reason for any lack of success is an excuse or a lack of belief in your own ability. However, hand in hand with this always comes the other problem of accusation and condemnation. This is also another part of the reason why people do not succeed in life. Without any doubt, anyone can blame their problems on other people, but failures make this a continual habit. "I drink because my wife cheated on me", "I look bad because my husband does not love me", "I lost my job because my boss is an idiot..." In these people's understanding, all their troubles have been caused by everyone around them. These people always say, "It was not my fault." This is a problem that is destroying them and their calling and success. The person who wants to have victory in life will always find strength within himself, when he has made a mistake to say, "I was wrong, I sinned, and fell..."

However, even if someone did actually become the cause of your problem, it should not affect your life. This is because as soon as you begin to blame someone for your lack of success, believe me, your life will begin to head downward. If there is somebody to blame, then there is an excuse for your humiliation, depression, and inactivity. Maybe, you could keep making progress but when condemnation, self-pity, and hatred toward the offender flood your heart, you will not even notice when you begin to do appalling things. You cannot begin to imagine how many women became prostitutes because they were raped once and how many men became homosexual because somebody interfered with them in their childhood, and how many people became criminals, alcoholics, and homeless just because somebody treated them unjustly. However, this is not an excuse to self-destruct. You personally, not your offender, will have to carry the burden of your own sin and your improper way of life regardless of whom and what was the cause of it. The quickest path to failure is to blame someone for what is happening in your life. The last thing you should do is to accuse someone by pointing your finger at them. Understand that you alone are responsible for your life and your problems. Your parents, spouse, the government, and the president are not responsible. You alone are responsible for your life.

Apart from simply judging and accusing a person, you ruin your life and you also practically become the murderer of the person that you are accusing. Jesus warned us about this danger.

"But I say to you that whoever is angry with his brother without a cause shall be in danger of the judgment. And whoever says to his brother, 'Raca!' shall be in danger of the council. But whoever says, 'You fool!' shall be in danger of hell fire."

Matthew 5:22

The brothers of Joseph for example, acted inhumanely because they began to see their younger brother as an enemy and the reason for their own lack of success. Condemnation that is hidden in your heart always leads to grave consequences.

Without question, people can sometimes be hideous to us. However, we have to let our hearts be free from any kind of offence. For example, what do we do if someone owes us money; do we demand it back from them? Yes, without a doubt, but without any kind of hatred and condemnation toward the person. We need to understand this. It is written: "Love your enemies." This means to continue to love people but at the same time demand justice. Otherwise, hatred will begin to devor you. For us not to destroy ourselves, it is important that we protect our hearts from any offence and hatred. Do you know what can help us achieve this? Having a high and attainable goal and being focused on it. Excuses and justifications, offence and hatred are mainly a part of someone who has no aim in life and who is not moving toward a goal. If you are occupied with a certain idea and its fulfillment then you simply will have no time or desire to think about what somebody said to you or why somebody looked at you in a certain way. Why bother? You will understand that all of this is meaningless compared to the goal you are heading toward. A great idea from God is the best form of protection against excuses, offence, and hatred. Do you have this in your life? If you do not, then you should definitely set yourself a task that will totally consume you and grip your soul from within, and which will help you to move forward while overlooking the offence. This is exactly what helped Jesus Christ to fulfill His mission. He could have thought of numerous excuses to quit and be offended at those who persecuted Him and did not accept Him. However, the great goal of saving humanity helped Him to stand strong and complete the mission that had been planned by God.

DO NOT BE DECEIVED...

What else is keeping us from becoming successful in life? Often we make excuses for ourselves not just because we do not have any goals, tasks, or a vision but also because we live in self-deception and denial. For example, some believers say, "God has told me that I will be a millionaire or the president of the country." Glory to God! I then ask them this question, "What are you doing so that this can actually comes to pass in your life? Are you already active in a political party or have you started your own business?" The reply that I hear is, "No I am a believer. God Himself will open the doors for me and bring the necessary people across my path..." This is real self-deception. Unfortunately, many people are hiding behind God like this with some kind of revelation but they are not taking the necessary actions to bring it to pass. They are waiting for manna to fall from heaven. while life goes on. For instance, why are some people not yet married? Is it because they are waiting for the perfect partner in life? If this is their reason then they are living an illusion. There are no perfect people. They do not exist at all in this world. Everyone has some fault in his character. Do not be deceived. Do you know why many of us like to live in self-deception? It is because it is very difficult and painful to acknowledge our mistakes or faults. However, I want to say to you that it is better to admit your faults than to live in self-deception.

FORGET THE PAST

What else keeps a person from becoming successful in life? In the previous chapter I mentioned this. However, now I want to stop and talk about this problem in more detail.

Let us look at one story written in the Book of Acts:

The next day, as they went on their journey and drew near the city, Peter went up on the housetop to pray, about the sixth hour. Then he became very hungry and wanted to eat; but while they made ready, he fell into a trance and saw heaven opened and an object like a great sheet bound at the four corners, descending to him and let down to the earth. In it were all kinds of four-footed animals of the earth, wild beasts, creeping things, and birds of the air. And a voice came to him, "Rise, Peter; kill and eat." But Peter said, "Not so, Lord! For I have never eaten anything common or unclean." And a voice spoke

to him again the second time, "What God has cleansed you must not call common." This was done three times. And the object was taken up into heaven again. Now while Peter wondered within himself what this vision which he had seen meant, behold, the men who had been sent from Cornelius had made inquiry for Simon's house, and stood before the gate. And they called and asked whether Simon, whose surname was Peter, was lodging there. While Peter thought about the vision, the Spirit said to him, "Behold, three men are seeking you. Arise therefore, go down and go with them, doubting nothing; for I have sent them."

Acts 10:9-20

What is this story about and what does it teach us? God called Peter to be the first preacher of the Gospel among the Gentiles. Up until that moment he had already done a lot in spreading the Good News of salvation among his own people, the Jews. However, when God called him to go further in order to carry out his purpose to the fullest, he did not answer God's call. The reason for this was his former life and his past. As a Jew, he could not turn away from the traditions of his people. "Not so, Lord! For I have never eaten anything common or unclean" — he replied to God. However, God tried to help Peter a few times to turn away from his past.

Unfortunately, Peter could not free himself from the past and from the fact that he was a Jew. Do you know what happened? God was forced to find another man in order to fulfill this mission. This man was Saul who we know as the apostle Paul.

Peter's life is demonstrative of another problem, which is, our past could stand in our path. God knows this. Therefore when we are reconciled to our Heavenly Father we receive salvation, and God teaches us to leave our past behind.

Therefore, if anyone is in Christ, he is a new creation; old things have passed away; behold, all things have become new.

2 Corinthians 5:17

OUR FOCUS SHOULD BE ON THE FUTURE.

Why did God make the decision to completely free us from the past? Because our past will hinder us from fulfilling our calling as we can see in the case of apostle Peter. If we are living in the past then we are continually looking back in our minds and we cannot go forward. Therefore if you are in Christ Jesus, you begin life with a clean sheet, and a new account starting from today as if it was the very first day of your life. This is also very important because when we were without God our life was built on worldly thinking. The foundation of our lives was built on tradition and religion and we had absolutely nothing in common with God's way of thinking. We built our lives independently from God's plans and intentions, but God says,

"For I know the thoughts that I think toward you, says the LORD, thoughts of peace and not of evil, to give you a future and a hope"

Jeremiah 29:11

If this is so, then if we go along our own path without looking at God, we will make many mistakes. In order to free each new believer from the burden of past mistakes and disappointments, He says, "I create all things new." What does this mean? It means that God forgets everything that has happened in our past. If we can also erase from our memories everything from the past and start from scratch then we will have a one hundred percent chance of becoming successful in life and achieving all that God has called us to do in this life. Therefore forget the past and begin to live in the present!

However, when I say "the past" I do not mean just the bad things in your past but also the good things. This is very important. If you have some achievements, success, or things you are proud of in your past, then beware! The devil will use these things against you. At a difficult time he will use them against you. This is because even though we want to forget about those sinful things we did in the past, at the same time we also want to continually dwell mentally on the positive things in our past. If you are a Christian, then at those times in your life when you are going through a desert or facing a major problem, the devil will begin to remind you of how good life used to be in Egypt so that you will suddenly desire to go back to the world of sin.

I thought about this for a long time. Do you know why Paul did not have the same problems that Peter and many other disciples of Jesus encountered in their lives? I found the answer to this question in the book of Philippians, where the apostle Paul said,

Brethren, I do not count myself to have apprehended; but one thing I do, forgetting those things which are behind and reaching forward to those things which are ahead, I press toward the goal for the prize of the upward call of God in Christ Jesus.

Philippians 3:13,14

But what things were gain to me, these I have counted loss for Christ. Yet indeed I also count all things loss for the excellence of the knowledge of Christ Jesus my Lord, for whom I have suffered the loss of all things, and count them as rubbish, that I may gain Christ...

Philippians 3:7,8

Pay attention to what Paul considered to be worthless. These are the things that he had before considered to be advantageous. These were success, money, and position in society or in other words, absolutely everything in his past. That is why while Peter was busy struggling with his past, Paul was focused on the future and therefore, he was able to live in total freedom and fulfill his calling.

Erase from your life your past: both the good things and the bad. Do not remember the past and your former way of thinking. Meditate only on the calling that God placed in your spirit and then neither the devil, hell, nor the world will be able to stop you. Let God become your strength and power. Let God become your inspiration and energy. You can do all things in Christ Jesus! Just try to move forward, work on yourself and labor diligently. Refuse to allow any excuses to be found in your heart and mind that you cannot do something or receive something then God will definitely help you, and you will surely become the person that God wants you to be. Do not be a failure who justifies his inactivity, or a person who can find millions of reasons to refuse God's plan for his life. It is better to believe God and focus on the fact that everything will work out for you. Then you will definitely see positive results.

GOLDEN TRUTHS

• The reason why a person does not have success can be found inside him. It is his worldview, conscience, and perception of life.

• A high and attainable goal and being focused on it, is the best cure for laziness, excuses, offence, and hatred.

• It is better to admit your failure than to live in self deception.

• Total freedom from your past; both the good and the bad things is the foundation for a successful life.

CHAPTER 4

HOW TO USE OPPORTUNITIES

Another reason why people fail to be successful is because they are blind to the opportunities that God gives to them every day and therefore they do not seize them.

Much food is in the fallow ground of the poor

Often you hear people say that life is not fair. On one hand this could be true. However, if you look at it from another angle, there is a God and He is a just God. He gives absolutely every person the opportunity to be successful in life. This is a truth that we must realize and never forget. We must always keep this in our mind. The only question now is what will be done with these opportunities, how will they be used, or will they be used at all? In the book of Proverbs it is written:

Much food is in the fallow ground of the poor, and for lack of justice there is waste.

Proverbs 13:23

What do the words "much food" means? It means many opportunities. Every day God offers us certain opportunities. From this Scripture we can see that even if a person is poor, he still has the opportunity of having a significant amount of bread on his table, or in other words, to be successful in life. In the same way God sends the sun and rain on the rich and the poor, is the same way He gives opportunities to each and every person. He does not deprive anyone of his rights. He never shows favoritism. However, why is it that very often the poor continues to be poor? It is because they simply cannot see and do not pay any attention to the opportunities which God gives to them every day in many different forms. All sorts of ideas could arise during a time of prayer, or important information from a conversation with someone or from a book could be obtained, and many other things of a similar nature.

There are hidden opportunities every place and in everything. Every day! If you believe that the steps of the righteous are ordered by the Lord, as it is written in the Bible, "I have taught you in the way of wisdom; I have led you in right paths" (Proverbs 4:11), then you should remember that no meeting, conversation, or situation happens by chance. God allows all things so that we can use these opportunities for our own good. However, unfortunately we only see in part, we look but we do not see and we listen but we do not understand.

Think about who you met yesterday. Why did you not call somebody today? Why did you not inquire about the project that somebody was working on? Maybe this was exactly what you needed to do, and so on...

Very often we miss opportunities because we rely on ourselves and on our own ability. We consider ourselves to be important people and wise in our own eyes. However, when we rely on our own strength then God's opportunities become inaccessible to us. It is written in the Bible:

"Ask, and it will be given to you; seek, and you will find; knock, and it will be opened to you."

Matthew 7:7

What does this scripture teach us? In order to use the opportunities it is important to learn how to ask questions and knock on closed doors. Many people are not able to do this simply because of pride and "ego." Instead of asking somebody about the topic they are interested in, those people are tormented with the fear of what other people might think of them and how they will react to their questions. As a consequence, opportunities slip pass these people.

Therefore the first and most essential condition needed to see and use the opportunities, is humility and turning away from your "ego." Learn to search for opportunities. Learn to ask, knock, press in, and demand from life in order to receive the opportunities and the chance to be successful!

The second very important condition that is necessary in order for you not to miss your opportunities, is hard work and the ability to be constantly engaged in concrete and constructive work. This will help you to acquire more knowledge and skills and widen your social sphere. This consequently will increase the number of your opportunities. Therefore, develop within yourself the habit of work.

Always do more than is required of you and then God will give you such opportunities that you could not have even dreamed of.

Applying diligence to our work ethics is another key that will open opportunities before us. We should not work only when we feel like it. For example, today I want to work and tomorrow I do not want to work. If we want to be successful then we need to continually work and be consistent every day and not slow our work tempo. Every day we should increase our professionalism at work more and more. We must keep focused on becoming perfect in all our affairs. Do not stop achieving things. Then God will definitely present before you some kind of opportunity that will raise you up to the next level of success. He always rewards patient, diligent, and stable people who are skilled in their work.

FOR WHO HAS DESPISED THE DAY OF SMALL THINGS?

Another factor that reveals the reason why people do not see their opportunities is their attempt to get everything here and now in larger and larger quantities...

Why for example, does the problem of prostitution exist? This is because many of these young girls want to acquire beautiful things and look glamorous, seemingly without any effort at all. At first this works for them. However, after a couple of years of this type of work they begin to look awful. Nearly all prostitutes become drug addicts and alcoholics because it is not easy to live in continual humiliation and experience physical and emotional rape, and at the same time maintain a sober mind and a clear memory.

This is the price they have to pay in the pursuit of a deceitfully easy beautiful life.

Life will always find a way of teaching its lesson to those who want to have wealth, fame, and recognition without any sort of effort. This is why the prisons are full of people. Three quarters of all people in prison are thieves and robbers. These are people who wanted to have as much blessing as possible and to become the masters of life by taking a path without any humility, work, and service to people. Instead they took the path of violence and deception.

Many people do not want to be patient, work, and wait. Everyone wants miracles. However, the truth of life is that everything great requires work and patience. Great things are not born right away. All great things begin from something small. Therefore, do not neglect small beginnings. Everything small that now seems to be nothing and insignificant has the potential for growth. Everything small is relational. Therefore, even if God has promised us something great and wonderful, we should not disdain small and insignificant business. This is because only by proving our faithfulness in something small can God give us those thing He has promised us, and bigger things. This is the only way things work in life: from small to big, and from simple to complicated. For example, how did a forest begin? It came from a small seed. From whom did the population of this earth of over 6 billion people start? From only two people, Adam and Eve.

Remember that God always begins from something small. If we have the right attitude to the small thing then it will begin to grow and become great in the end.

Based on what has been said here, what conclusions can we draw?

First of all, every day God gives us opportunities. Sometimes they are so small and insignificant in our eyes that we just pass them by. We are waiting for something great. We think that insignificant things should not distract us. Our great expectations do not allow us to see the small opportunities that the Lord sends to us every day.

Secondly, in order to see great things in your life, you have to be faithful first in the little things, and thank God for even the most insignificant blessings. If we will be faithful in little, then God will be faithful to us in much. However, a lot of people neglect the small beginning be-cause it seems to them not attractive and worthy of their full attention. However, God likes to use unattractive and insignificant things to test our hearts. Remember the story of the birth of Jesus Christ. He is the King of kings and the Savior of the world but He began His life's journey not in a king's palace but in a manger.

Usually people who consider themselves too important to do something insignificant are in actual fact small and unimportant on the inside. They simply cannot do something insignificant. Therefore, on a large scale they are not worthy to receive the great blessing that is hidden behind the small things. Do not try to be recognized in something great immediately. Start with something small.

For who has despised the day of small things?

Zechariah 4:10

Successful people are only successful because they pay attention to details and are focused on seemingly insignificant facts. They can be faithful in little things.

WHOEVER IS GREATEST AMONG YOU SHOULD BECOME THE LEAST

Why do most people neglect the little things? It is because they are focused on themselves and on what they can get and not on what they can give. They do not want to share their time, nice words, advice, and smile with other people. Very often big opportunities are hiding behind something insignificant in the form of serving other people. God is looking for such people who can humble themselves and become servants so that they can then become the first, after becoming the last.

The one true path to real promotion comes when we humble ourselves and begin to give ourselves to other people and serve them. This must be a central focus for us. However, if you have no desire to be a servant then you will never be able to become someone great.

Remember the men of God in the Bible: Joseph, Daniel, and Moses. All of them took the path of servant hood before they became rulers. They were faithful servants in somebody else's business. Even God Himself could not avoid this law of life,

...Who, being in the form of God, did not consider it robbery to be

equal with God, but made Himself of no reputation, taking the form of a bondservant, and coming in the likeness of men. And being found in appearance as a man, He humbled Himself and became obedient to the point of death, even the death of the cross.**

Philippians 2:6-8

Only after Jesus took upon Himself the form of a bondservant did God promote Him and gave Him the Name which is above all other names.

Therefore God also has highly exalted Him and given Him the name which is above every name, that at the name of Jesus every knee should bow, of those in heaven, and of those on earth, and of those under the earth, and that every tongue should confess that Jesus Christ is Lord, to the glory of God the Father.

Philippians 2:9-11

FAITHFUL IN LITTLE IS FAITHFUL IN MUCH

Learn to be a servant and to be faithful in the little things. Otherwise, as it is written in the Gospel of Luke:

"And if you have not been faithful in what is another man's, who will give you what is your own?"

Luke 16:12

If you do not, at sometime prove yourself to be faithful in someone else's business for example, in your leadership, or in the affairs of your colleagues, even if nobody has asked you to do it, or nobody is thankful for it, do not expect God to give you some great work for you to carry out.

Only by being conscientious and responsible in somebody else's business will the doors for your successful future open.

Why is it so essential to be faithful in someone else's business and in little? This is because:

"He who is faithful in what is least is faithful also in much; and he who is unjust in what is least is unjust also in much."

Luke 16:10

Please understand that above all, God is not looking for some hero or giant that can show big and great things. He is looking for people who will be conscientious and faithful in the smallest of things. This is because only such people will be able to deal with large and difficult tasks.

On the basis of this, begin to carry out the most insignificant tasks with excellence and diligence, take the simplest jobs, not the most prestigious and do the job with your whole heart even if you have to do it for free. Then you will see what God will do.

When the topic of being faithful in little is raised, some believers complain, "How can I be faithful to an unbelieving boss? He is a sinner." It is not important to whom we are faithful in small things, whether he is righteous or a sinner because, "...if you have not been faithful in the unrighteous mammon, who will commit to your trust the true riches?" (Luke 16:11).

For God, it is important that we are faithful and righteous, so that we do our work honestly and conscientiously with our whole heart as if unto the Lord despite everything around us. That is what is required of us. God will deal with the rest.

GOLDEN TRUTHS

- God gives absolutely everybody the opportunity to be successful in life.
- There are hidden opportunities for each person everywhere and in everything, every day!
- When we rely on our own strength, God's opportunities become inaccessible to us.
- Therefore the first and most essential attribute required to see and use the opportunities is humility and turning away from our "ego."
- Always do more than is required of you and then God will give you such opportunities that you have never dreamed of before.
- Do not stop attaining goals.
- If we are faithful in little things then God will be faithful to us in big things.
- The only path to real promotion is to humble yourself and make yourself of no reputation and then begin to give yourself to other people and serve them.

CHAPTER 5

HOW TO MANAGE YOURSELF

From all that has been said in the previous chapters it is possible to draw the conclusion that the reason for a lack of success is hidden, above anything else, within us. The fundamental reason for all of our misfortune lies within us, or in other words, in our ego.

GOD RESISTS THE PROUD

Let us look at the reason why Satan was thrown into hell. In the Book of Isaiah it is written that:

"How you are fallen from heaven, O Lucifer, son of the morning! How you are cut down to the ground, you who weakened the nations! For you have said in your heart: 'I will ascend into heaven, I will exalt my throne above the stars of God; I will also sit on the mount of the congregation on the farthest sides of the north; I will ascend above the heights of the clouds, I will be like the Most High.' Yet you shall be brought down to Sheol, to the lowest depths of the pit."

Isaiah 14:12-15

From this Scripture it is clear that pride was the reason for the fall of

Satan. When we lift ourselves higher than God and are full of ourselves then we are no longer serving God, but ourselves. However, as we see from the story of Lucifer, this is a very dangerous path. Please remember that pride and ego can destroy anyone. Regardless of how anointed you may be, as soon as you begin to be proud, and lift yourself up, then the same God Who blessed you and raised you up, will be the same One Who will fight against you. Who is ready to fight with God? Do not try it! It is a terrifying thing! It is a battle you cannot win. Lucifer the son of the morning was chosen and anointed by God. However, despite this, God was forced to resist him and as we see, it ended horribly for Satan.

We all need to be simply aware that in this life we are our own greatest enemy. Unfortunately in these last days, this enemy will attack the children of God and the Church. Apostle Paul warns us about this,

But know this, that in the last days perilous times will come: For men will be lovers of themselves, lovers of money, boasters, proud, blasphemers, disobedient to parents, unthankful, unholy...

2 Timothy 3:1,2

Loving one-self (the lust of the flesh) is the first signal that we are living in the last days. Unfortunately, today we can see this happening everywhere. We can see more and more that people are simply obsessed with themselves, "I have to make a career for myself, I must make a lot of money, I should look better than everyone else..." I, I, I. This is all connected to the fact that the system of this world only recognizes successful people. If you are not prospering, then in the eyes of those around you, you are a nobody, just an empty space. However, if you are a high income earner and are prominent in society then that is a completely different thing. Of course, it is only natural that all people want to be valued and respected. We have talked earlier about what real success is but many do not understand its true meaning.

As a result they do all they can to reach the peak of success fame, popularity, and riches...What is more, many of these people in the pursuit of their own success, do not care about how many people they victimize along the way. Such people act in the same way as a cancer cell, which destroys everything around it as it grows more and more and spreads out over the entire body. Egocentric people use other people like a trampoline in order to reach their own goals. However, this contradicts God's principles. The Kingdom of God operates in this way; the anointed and chosen people of God are to help other people to come up to their own level and then make them kings and priests for the Lord. Therefore, check your own heart. What is your motivation for building a large church or earning lots of money for example? What is driving you? Do you want these things so that you can be rich and famous or so that through these things you can help to lift up other people around you? If you do not get your heart right in time, you may rise up to a certain level but then the time will come when you will inevitably fall; God will bring you down.

How is it possible to become a victim of pride? How can you protect yourself from pride? What do you focus your attention on when the temptation of pride and fame arises? Let us look at what Jesus did during these times. In the Gospel of John it is written:

Therefore when Jesus perceived that they were about to come and take Him by force to make Him king, He departed again to the mountain by Himself alone.

John 6:15

Jesus knew that the people wanted to make Him king. However, instead of joyfully accepting such an appealing proposition, He simply ran away and hid in the mountains. Why? Because He knew that if He agreed, then there would be no Golgotha and mankind would not have had the chance to be saved. We can draw a conclusion from this: a person who is obedient to God knows he did not come to this earth to build his own kingdom. He came to build God's Kingdom. Yes, of course when we serve God, He will raise us up and make us the head and not the tail. However, we should never try to raise ourselves up and make ourselves great and succumb to flattery and the praises from other people. The devil's tactics have never changed. Through flattery, the devil wants to distract each one of us from our own calling. Therefore, do not focus on yourself. This is the road to destruction. Instead, continue progressing toward God's goals. It was this attitude that helped Jesus to stand when Peter tried to talk Him out of His readiness to die.

And He began to teach them that the Son of Man must suffer many things, and be rejected by the elders and chief priests and scribes, and be killed, and after three days rise again. He spoke this word openly. And Peter took Him aside and began to rebuke Him. But when He had turned around and looked at His disciples, He rebuked Peter, saying, "Get behind Me, Satan! For you are not mindful of the things of God, but the things of men."

Mark 8:31-33

The ability of self control is one of the greatest victories in life.

THE GREAT POWER OF SELF-DISCIPLINE AND SELF-MANAGEMENT

What should we do in order to free ourselves from our ego and self-centeredness? First of all, we must endeavor to talk less about ourselves, our achievements, and victories. In this area as well as in many others, self-discipline can help a lot.

Let us look at what is written in the second Letter to the Corinthians:

For though He was crucified in weakness, yet He lives by the power of God. For we also are weak in Him, but we shall live with Him by the power of God toward you. Examine yourselves as to whether you are in the faith. Test yourselves. Do you not know yourselves, that Jesus Christ is in you?—unless indeed you are disqualified.

2 Corinthians 13:4,5

The spiritual world works in accordance with God's laws. Ignorance of these laws does not free you from any responsibility. In the same way you cannot be excused just because you do not know the physical and governmental laws. For example, if you took something out of your landlord's apartment without his permission, you would be charged with theft, even if you did not know this was a crime.

One of the spiritual laws says that a person who refuses to manage and discipline his own flesh will be disciplined and taught by life itself. If a person refuses to work on himself in the "secret place" then the world will have to fix him in a more brutal way. Only when you "crucify" your flesh can you be guaranteed life. Jesus knew this spiritual law and therefore He allowed Himself to be crucified in order to celebrate the victory of resurrection.

If we can crucify in ourselves every desire of the flesh and every deadly habit in the "secret place," then God will help us to triumph openly just like the resurrection of Jesus, which is celebrated all over the world.

Believers who do not smoke or drink and who live a righteous way of life, are considered to be weak. However, those who look at believers in this way, do not understand that a person who takes authority over himself and his weaknesses will in time, be glorified by God with His strength. "For we also are weak in Him, but we shall live with Him by the power of God toward you."

If we are hidden in God and we turn away from a sinful way of life then when the world is suffering and in torment, we will be protected by His strength. Pay attention to the fifth verse, "Examine yourselves as to whether you are in the faith. Test yourselves. Do you not know yourselves, that Jesus Christ is in you?—unless indeed you are disqualified."

Test yourself so that God will not have to test you. This is the law of nature. It does not depend on whether you are a believer or not, or whether you perceive the Bible as the Word of God or not. This law works for everyone without exception. If you will test yourself, then life will not destroy you. If you refuse to examine and judge yourself then you will only have yourself to blame. How often, for instance, have you talked to a person about the dangers of smoking, to be met with the reply, "I like smoking," and soon after that person is diagnosed with lung cancer. Or parents might say to their children, "Go to school, study well and live according to God's laws," but the children ignore the advice of their parents and later on in life, perhaps, when they are forty years old they become homeless. By refusing to examine ourselves and judge our actions, and discipline our flesh, we will sooner or later find ourselves in a place of suffering.

God did not give us the Bible in vain. This book opens unto us the principles and laws of life, thanks to which, we can understand the foundations on which the world stands, and how to live so we would enjoy life instead of being tormented by it. Everything that we have today is the result of whether we have obeyed the laws of life or not. Another one of these laws, the law of the flesh and the spirit says:

For if you live according to the flesh you will die; but if by the Spirit you put to death the deeds of the body, you will live.

Romans 8:13

What does it mean to live in the flesh? It means to live as you desire according to the ways of the world, without paying attention to God's laws. However, if you choose to take this path, then you cannot avoid the consequences and God clearly and openly warns us about this, "For if you live according to the flesh you will die..."

For example, why do people contract sexually transmitted diseases? It is because they refuse to discipline their flesh. We all have flesh, and it pressures each one of us and demands its own way. However, when we humble ourselves before God and try to live by His laws and go to church, He gives us the power and grace to master our flesh and overcome temptations.

For if you live according to the flesh you will die; but if by the Spirit you put to death the deeds of the body, you will live.

Romans 8:13

The words "put to death" could be translated as "discipline." If we learn to manage and discipline ourselves then we will really begin to live. I can recall that my African friends who came with me to study in the USSR developed the habit of smoking as a measure of keeping warm in winter. Then our Russian "friends" revealed to us another "secret": vodka, which supposedly keeps you even warmer in winter! I was continually teased but I had made up my mind to be different from my friends and decided not to smoke or drink. I had unwaveringly chosen not to indulge in the desires of my flesh and that is why today, I have life and life to the fullest. Many of my colleagues have since died from alcoholism because they made excuses for their flesh. The flesh will always find an excuse!

THE PAIN OF SELF-DISCIPLINE

Resisting the flesh and the accusations and mocking from those around you is always unpleasant and painful. I now want to share with you another spiritual law. It appears to be that each one of us without exception will have to go through specific pain, but this pain can be divided into two types. The first type of pain is the pain of selfdiscipline. This pain came to test me when I was mocked and became the butt of my friends' jokes because I did not drink or smoke. Instead of going out with girls and having a good time, I sat in a library all day and immersed myself in my studies. I did not try to escape this pain, and now it has passed. However, my fellow students that were unwilling to endure the pain of self-discipline are now experiencing an even worse pain. Life is dealing with them with the cruel blows of prison, poverty, hangovers, and withdrawal symptoms from drugs. This illustration clearly demonstrates that the pain of self-discipline is nothing more than a little scratch.

We cannot avoid pain in life and can only decide on the kind of pain we want to endure. It will either be the pain of self-discipline that will in the end reward us, or the pain of life when it crushes us. Only then will we regret not disciplining ourselves earlier. Therefore test yourselves, and judge yourselves. Become disciplined now, or life will force you to do it later anyway. This is a law.

Do you know it really surprises me when young girls and women try to get a job as a secretary or a cleaner? I think to myself, "These girls are only twenty five years old. Go and pay the price of having an education and change your profession because even if you do manage to find a job as a secretary now, in ten years time a young eighteen- year-old girl with long legs will replace you. Where will you go then without an education?" The law of life is like this. You should already be considering and planning for your retirement. Everyone should be preparing for old age now. Do you want your old age to be blessed and secured? Then that means you need to be proactive today. Get educated in one or two areas and in twenty years time you will enjoy life. Maybe you think this is too difficult. Ultimately, the choice is yours. You can choose to not pay the price now and avoid difficulties and pain, but do not be fooled, in twenty years time life will still teach you, and then the real pain will begin. Everyone knows that pain is more endurable in youth than in old age. If a nineteen year old breaks his arm, it will heal and not cause any trouble, but if a sixty year old breaks their arm it will be a different story. Therefore endure the pain while you are still young. Endure the pain today and do not defer it to tomorrow. Wage your war today. Get an education today. Do your business today. Overcome smoking today. Secure the victory over alcoholism today. Otherwise, if you postpone the battle to another day you will become crippled for the rest of your life.

Test your own path right now and pull yourself together. Ask God to help you. However, if you refuse to make the decision to discipline yourself then God Himself will look at you and say, "He is not good for anything."

Do not underestimate the power of self-discipline and self-management. It is the law of the flesh and the spirit. Let us focus on the law of the spirit to avoid being tormented by the consequences of the law of the flesh.

The skeleton of success is self-discipline. If there is a skeleton then the skin will not have a problem. However, if the skeleton is missing then it matters not how many kilograms of flesh there is, it will all collapse. The foundation of success is self-discipline. What does this mean? For example, if a young man decides to start a business and in the course of several years he becomes a millionaire; that is great! Well done! However, there could be a concern here. If during this time the young man did not conquer the flesh then this man will find himself drawn toward alcoholism and adultery. In this scenario what do you think will happen to him a few years later? These fatal habits will destroy him because the flesh always craves for more. The more success he achieves, while his flesh is not subjected to his control, the more the flesh will dictate to him and the strong urges will control him. Usually the people who live a life in the flesh say, "I am in control of the situation, if I want to drink, I drink, and if I do not, I will not." When you are nobody this is not so serious. However, when you begin to climb the ladder of success, this becomes a serious matter. With the arrival of money and success the flesh takes over and if the person has not learned self-discipline, he will fall. If he does not get a hold of himself in time then pain and regret gloatingly wait for him. I see this every single day.

A PERSON WITH SELF-CONTROL IS BETTER THAN

A PERSON WHO TAKES A CITY

Begin to pay the price for self-discipline and self-control today. Declare war on the areas in yourself that need changing because "He who is slow to anger is better than the mighty, and he who rules his spirit than he who takes a city" (Proverbs 16:32).

Why is someone who can control himself better than someone who takes a city? This is because if you conquer a city, but cannot control yourself you will eventually lose that city. Then what was the use of taking it? The one who has overcome his flesh is better than any record breaker. Recently in England one of the greatest soccer players of his time, George

Best died. He still had many years left to live, but the works of the flesh destroyed him. The fact is that after a match he liked to relax by drinking a little, and in the end this fatal habit killed him. Unfortunately, neither his titles nor his millions could save him. If the flesh is not overcome then it can destroy power, anointing, and talent. This is exactly what happened to the Bible hero Samson. His weakness was with women, and the lust of his eyes destroyed him.

Then the Philistines took him and put out his eyes, and brought him down to Gaza. They bound him with bronze fetters, and he became a grinder in the prison.

Judges 16:21

Samson refused to discipline his eyes and as a result his enemies plucked them out. From this we can draw the conclusion that, what we fail to discipline will become a problem for us in the future. Samson failed to pay the price of self-discipline and as a consequence suffered an even greater pain. Therefore, it is not what you can do that is the most important thing or whether you are heroic (and Samson without a doubt was a real hero), it is a question of how much you can be patient and control yourself. To be a hero in the eyes of people is good, but first of all you need to have the victory over yourself and your inner man. Compromise is something that needs to be overcome. More than often it is compromise that leads us away from our calling and prevents us from being successful.

Every day we run into things and people that ask us to step out of our plans and try to lead us away from our main objectives. This is where the war breaks out. It is a war against pressing issues and urgent demands. However, in order to have victory in this war it is essential that you be very disciplined. When you are victorious over yourself and compromise then you can look people straight in the eye and say with boldness, "Sorry but I cannot do that right now." Many people do not succeed because they do not want to fight against compromise in their own lives. The desire to be nice to everyone and please everyone destroys people, especially believers. If you do not learn to fight for your principles then someday by pleasing everyone, you will lose your own wife, children, husband, or business. To avoid this catastrophe, we have to be people of principle with the ability to fight for them.

People often ask me, "How do you find the time to do everything?" The answer is simple; it is by following my own principles. For example, in order to keep my family together, I have to be home on certain days and at certain times, no matter what. In order to keep my close relationship with God, I have to spend a certain amount of time with Him. I have consultations with people only on Mondays. If you did not manage to see me for consultation this Monday, I love you and I want to help you but you will have to wait until the next Monday. This is because I have only planned to use Mondays for consultations. If I were to react to every request outside my principles and planning schedule I would simply die, and be of no use to anyone. Therefore, it is imperative that we learn to be firm and not be too emotional or frivolous in relation to our basic principles. Otherwise, our lives will not be beneficial to us or to the people around us.

GOLDEN TRUTHS

• When we exalt ourselves higher than God then we are no longer serving Him, but ourselves.

• The greatest enemy of any person is his own ego.

• Never be focused on yourself.

• A person who refuses to manage himself and discipline his flesh will be disciplined and taught by life itself.

• Test yourself so that later God will not have to test you.

• Pain in life is inevitable.

• The skeleton of success is self-discipline.

• If your flesh is not submitted to you, then it will defeat power, anointing, and talent.

• Many people do not succeed because they do not want to fight against compromise.

CHAPTER 6

LET YOUR "YES" BE A "YES"...

In this chapter, I want to continue the topic of the previous chapter and talk about how important it is when you are on the path to success, to live righteously and be faithful to your word. This is another part of our life that requires self-discipline.

Unfortunately, many people do not take what they say and what they promise seriously. In Ukraine this is a major problem. People place little or no value on their words. They do not understand that each word carries weight and brings either life or death. It should not be like this.

BE PERFECT,

AS YOUR HEAVENLY FATHER IS PERFECT

In ancient times a promise was sealed with an oath. The oath forced a person to be faithful to his word, in order to carry out what he had said.

Again you have heard that it was said to those of old, 'You shall not swear falsely, but shall perform your oaths to the Lord.'

Matthew 5:33

Today an oath is a written contract, which compels a person to keep his word, gives weight to the promise and forces him to act more responsibly. However Jesus says:

"...But I say to you, do not swear at all: neither by heaven, for it is God's throne; nor by the earth, for it is His footstool; nor by Jerusalem, for it is the city of the great King. Nor shall you swear by your head, because you cannot make one hair white or black. But let your 'Yes' be 'Yes,' and your 'No,' 'No.' For whatever is more than these is from the evil one."

Matthew 5:34-37

What does the Lord want to get to us through these words? Our lives should be so crystal clear that no one could doubt our words. Anyone should be able to say, "If that person has promised then that means he will definitely do what he has said." Our lives should be straightforward. We should not have to convince anyone that we will do what we have promised. All of our convincing, excuses and proofs of our honesty, order and punctuality are what Jesus meant when he said: "For whatever is more than these is from the evil one."

If you are a Christian then you simply do not have a choice than to live and act honestly. Do you know why? The reason is simple. It is found in the forty-fifth verse of the same chapter. It is written there, "...that you may be sons of your Father in heaven..."

What does this mean? This means if you have accepted Jesus Christ as your Lord and Savior and you go to church, then you are not just a person, born of other people. Now you are born of God, your Heavenly Father. All parents want their children to be like them. God is not an exception. He wants us to be perfect just like He is (see Matthew 5:48). If God says to us,

"..let your 'yes' be a 'yes' and your 'no' be a 'no'," it is only because God is like this Himself.

A God of truth and without injustice.

Deuteronomy 32:4

Indeed, let God be true but every man a liar. As it is written, "That You may be justified in Your words, and may overcome when You are judged."

Romans 3:4

God is faithful, by whom you were called into the fellowship of His Son, Jesus Christ our Lord.

1 Corinthians 1:9

What does the word "faithful" mean? Faithful means that you do not change. God is not like a wavering leaf. He is sturdy. This means that even after ten or a hundred or a thousand years, He will still be the same. That is why we can turn to His Word, which was written more than two thousand years ago and receive healing, salvation, help, mercy, and forgiveness. His Word works even today only because God Himself is faithful. He also wants us to be faithful. He wants His children to be trustworthy, faithful, and responsible. He does not want our words to differ from our actions. He is waiting for us to finally become like Jesus. Who is Jesus Christ? He is the Son of God and the first born from among the children of God.

...And from Jesus Christ, the faithful witness, the firstborn from the dead, and the ruler over the kings of the earth. To Him who loved us and washed us from our sins in His own blood.

Revelation 1:5

Jesus is the first born of many millions of brethren that have been adopted by God.

For whom He foreknew, He also predestined to be conformed to the image of His Son, that He might be the firstborn among many brethren.

Romans 8:29

Why is He the firstborn? This is because no one had ever become a child of God before Jesus. No one had ever been born of the Heavenly Father before this time. No one had known His character. Jesus was the first to reveal the Father to us. He also clearly showed us how all the children of God are to live and act. However, He led a clean and transparent life and as we can see from the Scriptures He was not a hypocrite. There was not one bit of falsehood in Him. His yes, always meant yes, (see 2 Corinthians 1:19).

At no time did He act one way in front of His disciples and another way in front of Pilate, the Sadducees, and the Pharisees. He was true to Himself, and His word even in the face of death. The first apostles understood this lesson well. This is shown clearly by the words of the apostle Paul:

Therefore, when I was planning this, did I do it lightly? Or the things I plan, do I plan according to the flesh, that with me there should be Yes, Yes, and No, No? But as God is faithful, our word to you was not Yes and No. For the Son of God, Jesus Christ, who was preached among you by us — by me, Silvanus, and Timothy — was not Yes and No, but in Him was Yes. For all the promises of God in Him are Yes, and in Him Amen, to the glory of God through us.

2 Corinthians 1:17-20

ALL LIARS SHALL HAVE THEIR PART IN THE LAKE WHICH BURNS WITH FIRE AND BRIMSTONE.

Unfortunately, many of us believers desire to please everyone. We are afraid of spoiling our reputations and when we are pressured by circumstances, we turn from being the children of the Most High God into children of this present world. This deceitful and hypocritical attitude explains why man is not confident in himself or grounded in the truth. He does not know and understand who he is. However, remember that if you are born from above then you are a child of God. This title is better than anything else in this world. Therefore, do not betray Him no matter who is before you. Do not draw back from Him and do not be afraid to say that you are a believer and a child of the Living God! Do not think about what people will think about you or your reputation, as a Christian your reputation no longer belongs to you. You are dead to this present world and to all that is valuable in its eyes. The dead do not care about what people think and say about them. The most important thing is what God thinks about you. Focus on this truth and it will help you withstand any test.

Perhaps there is someone reading these lines that thinks that this is an absolutely impossible thing to do. However, if Christ lives in your heart then simply allow Him to live through you with His holiness and transparency and your life will be cleansed of all hypocrisy and deceit. Just hold Jesus close to you always, forget yourself and direct all your efforts toward pleasing God and not the world. The world system is not for us, the children of God. This is because the world belongs to the devil. That is why the children of this world do not understand Jesus and do not understand the children of God.

"...Why do you not understand My speech? Because you are not able to listen to My word. You are of your father the devil, and the desires of your father you want to do. He was a murderer from the beginning, and does not stand in the truth, because there is no truth in him. When he speaks a lie, he speaks from his own resources, for he is a liar and the father of it."

John 8:43,44

What does the "lusts of your father" mean? It means all kinds of different sins. Therefore, as soon as you begin to live according to the laws of this world you automatically reject your Heavenly Father and accept the devil as your father. If there is no righteousness, joy, love, and peace in your life, which are all attributes of God, then you are on a dangerous path. If you are constantly lying then you have become a child of darkness. It does not matter if the lie is "white" and meant for good because in God there is no falsehood or unrighteousness. There are no white lies and black lies. As it is written in the Book of Revelation:

"But the cowardly, unbelieving, abominable, murderers, sexually immoral, sorcerers, idolaters, and all liars shall have their part in the lake which burns with fire and brimstone, which is the second death."

Revelation 21:8

As you can see here, God does not divide lies into two categories, white lies and black lies. All deceivers and liars without exception will burn in hell fire. Therefore, if subject to circumstances, you deviate from the truth, and then comfort yourself by thinking that everything is going to be all right, you are acting like the father of lies the devil, which "...was a murderer from the beginning, and does not stand in the truth, because there is no truth in him. When he speaks a lie, he speaks from his own resources, for he is a liar and the father of it" (John 8:44).

What did the devil do? He did not stand for the truth. His children are the same. There is no truth in the children of this world. Think for a moment about your unbelieving friends. You tell them, for example, "It is wrong for you to live in civil marriage. It is a sin." however, they reply like this, "This is just the way life is... We are in love... Everyone lives like this now" — as the scripture says, they fulfill the "lusts of their father." The Word of God is not an authority for them. Therefore do not imitate anyone in this world and constantly test yourself to see if you are standing in the truth and walking in it. Are you free from the sins that your Father God freed you from when you came to Him in repentance? Do you remember that He saved you so you would be a light to your relatives and those around you and, fast and pray for them to spend eternity with God? If you do not stand in the truth, then not only your relatives but you also will burn in hell. That is why Jesus clearly said, "...let your 'yes' be a 'yes' and your 'no' be a 'no'." He knew who the Father of lies was and did not want His children to have anything to do with deception. Let your life be pure, transparent, and clear. Let every word that falls from your lips carry weight. Let your "yes" be a "yes" and your "no" be a "no". This will really help you to keep your focus on what you are doing.

NOT MY WILL BUT YOUR WILL BE DONE

A person who is focused on his calling can say "no," because he does not care if people will stop fellowshipping with him, curse, criticize, or laugh at him. His main goal is not to please people but to fulfill the will of God for his life.

Believe me that when you really begin to focus on your work, you will be ready to look people in the eye and say, "I really respect you, but my answer is 'no'." Moreover, you should be able to say "no" not only to bad and inappropriate deals but also, more importantly to good ones. Even people you like and have dreamed about all your life could get you off track. This is very hard but if you are able to control your flesh and die to yourself for the sake of the will of God then you are really already a great person. This is how Joseph and Daniel acted. Jesus also acted this way. He really wanted to live, He did not want to die young, but He was able to say "no" to His desires.

"...Father, if it is Your will, take this cup away from Me; nevertheless not My will, but Yours, be done."

Luke 22:42

This prayer is for all of us. May God give us the power and grace to say "no" to the things that we like but are ungodly. May He strengthen us when we have the desire to give in and allow the flesh to have its way, and when attractive propositions try to lure us away from God's plan.

This is because when we can say "no" to those who we like, then we can expect to receive something much better. It is written: ".good and acceptable and perfect will of God" (Romans 12:2).

Therefore learn to say "no" to the good and advantageous, in order to receive the best. For this you have to keep your focus and not become weak.

GOLDEN TRUTHS

• Our lives should be so crystal clear that no one could doubt our words.

• All deceivers and liars without exception will burn in hell fire.

• If you are able to say "no" when it is convenient and inconvenient, and you can control your flesh and die to yourself for the sake of the will of God, then you are really already a great person.

• Learn to say "no" to the good and the advantageous, in order to receive the best.

CHAPTER 7

THE POWER OF A DECISION

As you can see, in order to be successful in life, it is very important to work on yourself and your character. Having the ability to make a decision and then following it through is also vitally important on the path to success.

I want you to pay close attention to this chapter. If you do not have an understanding of its importance and even more, its practical application then none of your dreams or plans will ever come to pass. This chapter is about the significance of making a decision in life and then carrying it out.

I do not have to be a prophet to know what will happen to you tomorrow. All I need to do is to look at what you are doing today and the decisions you are making.

YOU ALONE DECIDE WHERE YOU WILL BE TOMORROW

Everything that is happening to us today is simply the result of decisions that we made yesterday. That is to say, yesterday's decisions determine the situation that we are in today. For example, if a young girl decides to get married without the blessing of her parents and the marriage fails after a couple of years, on her tearful return to them they will have nothing else to say to her except, "Dearest daughter, we warned you…"

You probably know very well the famous story of the prodigal son in the Gospel of Luke:

"...But when he came to himself, he said, 'How many of my father's hired servants have bread enough and to spare, and I perish with hunger!' I will arise and go to my father, and will say to him, "Father, I have sinned against heaven and before you, and I am no longer worthy to be called your son. Make me like one of your hired servants." And he arose and came to his father. But when he was still a great way off, his father saw him and had compassion, and ran and fell on his neck and kissed him."

Luke 15:17-20

What does this parable teach us? More than anything else it teaches us that our decisions determine our destiny. If the prodigal son had not made the decision to return in repentance to his father, he would have died with the pigs he was feeding.

Decision is a very powerful word. The person who refuses to make decisions is the one who allows circumstances and other people to use him for their own advantage. If your life is not very successful today, then it is mainly the result of a lack of decision making. You can pray, go to church and do a multitude of things but if you do not make concrete decisions then change will not take place in your life. This is a habit which has many adverse consequences because the law of life says, if in the course of three years you stay in the same situation, at the same level; whether it is spiritually, mentally, financially or in any other sphere, then you begin to lose even what you had, in other words you begin to deteriorate. If you do not make an effort to improve your relationship with your spouse then in three years it could end in a serious conflict or divorce. You can choose to ignore this law but it will nonetheless continue to operate.

Every day we lose time that we can never regain. Every day... and do you know why? Often it is because we do not make any firm decision and even if we make a decision, many of us do not carry these decisions through. Having made a decision, it is necessary to start taking certain steps to fulfill the things conceived in our heart.

HAVING MADE A DECISION, BEGIN TO ACT

You should not just dream and pray and wait for something to happen. Yes, God does miracles. However, please do understand that if you want to become a millionaire then just praying is not enough. You have to go and work, start your own business and get the necessary information. This is the same in any sphere of life. Do you want to have a happy family? Then go and learn all you can about family relations and put that knowledge into action. Do you want a promotion? Then go and be a diligent and responsible worker and then you will have a "miracle." however, if you just hope and do nothing apart from praying and going to church, then you are living in deception!

The future will bring a breakthrough to those who not only make a decision today but also begin to take certain steps toward what they have planned. This is the law of getting results. Having made a decision, it is essential to reinforce it with concrete steps that will lead you to its fulfillment. Otherwise, you will not carry through with it because as you may have noticed, that ninety percent of the time as soon as you have made a decision, a millions obstacles will come to distract you from its fulfillment. Therefore, if you really want to carry out the decision you have made it is essential to act quickly. But unfortunately, very often instead of taking concrete steps, we to the contrary, forget about it or put it aside, thinking, "Tomorrow I will begin, I will start on Monday..." Many unsuccessful people are so not because they were stupid or they did not have any ideas, but because of this "sickness" of putting everything on hold until tomorrow. They do not have enough decisiveness, drive, and inner "aggression" which would allow them to fulfill what they had planned. Believers, in particular, suffer from this condition.

When people come to God they turn away from their own ambitions and stop seeking their own way. This is the right thing to do. However, you do not need to kill all the drive you had in the world, but be more zealous now in glorifying God. What does this mean? This means if you are now striving to be successful then you are not doing it for yourself but for God's sake. If you want to become rich then you are not doing this in order to satisfy your own flesh but instead, you are using these finances, to serve God and spread His Kingdom throughout the earth. Therefore keep this focus in everything you do.

The overwhelming majority of people who rule this world, who became millionaires, successful businessmen, famous actors, and social activists rose to this position by their positive inner aggression. This allowed them to narrow the gap between decision making and taking the con-crete action toward its fulfillment.

HOW TO COMPLETE A TASK

How do you increase or preserve your zeal until what you have started is complete? How do you decrease the time between when a decision is made and an action is taken? Here are a few tips.

Before anything else, when you make a decision to do something you need to deliberately surround yourself with things that will remind you of it every day. For example, you have made the decision to become a millionaire. In order for this to become a reality, it is essential to surround yourself with various books, seminars and teaching cassettes on this topic. Then your dream will always be before your eyes and you will be reminded of the necessity of reading and listening to these materials.

Apart from visual reminders, it is also important for your thoughts to be channeled on the matter. Prayer helps a lot with this. Every day, pray about the goal that you have set yourself. This will, in its own way, remind you of the decision you have taken.

Meditating on your goal and on ways of executing it is another method to keep you from "forgetfulness." In the Book of Joshua it is written:

"...This Book of the Law shall not depart from your mouth, but you shall meditate in it day and night, that you may observe to do according to all that is written in it. For then you will make your way prosperous, and then you will have good success."

Joshua 1:8

Through meditation, we not only remind ourselves about the decisions we have made but we also make ourselves richer and wiser. When we do this, several strategies for the fulfillment of our goals, program and plan of action, revelation from God, and new ideas will come into our thoughts. In other words, order will come to the decision that has been made. The ability to meditate is a great advantage. You will not become successful by just rushing around. Therefore, it is essential to periodically get alone so that nothing distracts your thoughts from what you have planned. Carve out for yourself time to pray, read, and meditate on information you have received. Also, cultivate the habit of writing down all the ideas and suggestions from God that will come to you during this time. Why is it so necessary to write everything down? In the Book of Habakkuk it is written:

Then the LORD answered me and said: "Write the vision and make it plain on tablets, that he may run who reads it. For the vision is yet for an appointed time; but at the end it will speak, and it will not lie. Though it tarries, wait for it; because it will surely come, it

will not tarry."

Habakkuk 2:2,3

It is important to document your ideas first of all, so you do not forget them. Anything that you do not write down, you will forget. It is a law. Secondly, a documented vision will help you to take some kind of concrete step every day toward the realization of your vision. This is the second essential condition necessary to narrow the gap between a decision taken and fulfilling it.

Every day it is crucial that you make, even if it is only small steps, toward your goal because each step is bringing you closer to it. For example, if your dream is to obtain a higher education then you should arm yourself with a prospectus that will give you the information about your specialty, the choice of places where you could study and the associated costs, and the entrance exams, if any, you will have to pass. Then if it is necessary, go and study preparatory courses. Every day, step by step, you will get closer to your goal. It is very important to understand that you cannot become a professor or a millionaire in one day. However, if you begin to gather together everything needed for the fulfillment of your dream then one day you will discover you have already attained your goal.

The third essential requirement for the fulfillment of a decision that has been made is to start studying in order to acquire all the necessary knowledge. This is like gasoline in a car, and will help you move toward the vision you have placed before yourself. By reading the appropriate literature you will discover certain facts that will inspire you to move forward and strengthen your decisiveness to fulfill your goal. For this, you begin with the Bible because it is the foundation of everything. With the help of the Word of God, you will avoid countless unpleasant situations and achieve, in a very little time what other people had been trying to do for years. You therefore need to carefully study what God's Word says about your dream. Do not doubt the fact that in the Word of God you can find the answer to any question. Apart from this, the Bible gives us a strong spirit and inner wholeness. However, just reading the Word of God is not enough. Revelations from God relating to your profession will not come to you from reading the Bible. You have to read other literature for this.

For example, Isaac Newton was a leading physician, who discovered the foundational laws of motion that the whole world now uses. However, it is also well known that he was a preacher. He had more biblical knowledge than scientific. If he had only read the Bible then he would not have acquired the education in physics, chemistry, or mathematics and would have been unable to comprehend what God was trying to reveal to Him concerning the physical laws. In a like manner, we should also be intensively focused on the field of our calling, then when we read the Bible together with an education in our discipline, for example, mathematics, medicine, or computer technology, we will begin to see these areas of knowledge through God's eyes, and the supernatural will happen: we will receive God's ideas leading to the progress of humanity.

Therefore besides the Bible, you must also study all the specialized literature. If you want to become a medical personnel, then a study of medical books leading to an education in medicine is a requirement. If it is your dream to be a businessman, politician or teacher then you should equip yourself with knowledge connected to the chosen area of expertise. A Biblical and a spiritual understanding combined with a scientific and physical understanding will help you become the best of the best in your sphere of work. This is what made Daniel from the Bible great. He studied the laws of the Bible but at the same time he did not reject the wisdom of the Babylonians. There is always some knowledge that is necessary for life therefore; you have to be in a constant search for this wisdom.

How do you inspire yourself to study? This is a very important question because not many of us like to do this. However, the more we know, the better it is for us. People who achieve great things in this life acknowledge the importance and necessity of their own intellectual growth. There is no need to force these people to study, unlike others who study only to pass an exam and get a diploma. Successful people are those who are dedicated to their own self-education. They do not improve themselves in order to boast of their wisdom and qualifications but they do it in their quest to find answers to the new questions that life is asking them and to uncover secrets. These people read with thirst. They believe that they cannot become perfected just by quietly sitting on what they already know. They are simply "obsessed" with equipping themselves educationally.

Understanding that we do not know everything yet should inspire us to read. Probably nobody on this earth could say he knows everything. However, in their sub-conscious mind, many people do actually believe they know everything. "I already know everything I need for this life," they argue. But this is deception. In reality nobody knows everything he needs to know. If you believe you do not need to study because perhaps, you have one or two or even three higher degrees, then you are deceived. The Word of God warns people who think like this:

And if anyone thinks that he knows anything, he knows nothing yet as he ought to know.

1 Corinthians 8:2

Therefore, never stop reaching for something greater. In fact, you can also obtain knowledge not only from books and the internet but also from other people. It is very important to recognize and realize this. It is a fact that every person without exception, regardless of his position or status in life, can be a source of essential knowledge for us. This is a very mature approach to life and will allow us to be psychologically open to receive wisdom from anybody. This is also very important because as strange as it may seem, the knowledge that will help us most of all in life always seems to come from somewhere unexpected. Therefore, you have an advantage if you are always ready to learn from anyone you meet along your path.

Obtaining knowledge is essential for the decision you have made to become a reality. However, we should not just read and study superficially; instead we must meticulously investigate the smallest detail in the area of our expertise, and try not to miss anything. Then the achievability of our goal would be fully possible. I really like the Scripture in Second Timothy, where the apostle Paul instructs his young disciple:

Be diligent to present yourself approved to God, a worker who does not need to be ashamed, rightly dividing the word of truth.

2 Timothy 2:15

These are wonderful words. In order to be approved you should study diligently and know your subject so well so that you can both boldly talk and teach people.

The next thing that can help you to narrow the gap between your decision making and fulfilling it, is the ability to look at every obstacle and hardship as the next step toward victory. Look at any problem encountered as a possible solution to turn the negative situation into positive energy and inspiration. I mentioned this in the previous chapters. It is necessary to talk about this and remind you of it again and again, because for you to realize your dream, it is essential that you learn how to correctly react to problems and trials.

Often we think that obstacles and problems hinder us but in actual fact these are the things that promote us. However, this is not usually seen immediately. Every obstacle in reality is a hidden step on the path to promotion. Any pressure or resistance is a signal that you are making a step forward. Therefore, on the path to your goal you will definitely suffer attacks that are intended to make you feel disappointed and extinguish your faith for victory. They are designed to make you stop what you have begun. It is important to realize that it is not the difficulties that are the key issue. As you have already understood the key issue is your reaction to them and your ability to turn your bad situation into your advantage, the ability to turn a negative situation into a positive and a minus into a plus. A minus could mean any problem. When we react to them with depression, tears, and disappointment we add another minus to the already negative situation, and with this we rob our life even more. However, when we react to a negative situation correctly we turn the minus into a plus. Why is a minus necessary? As you know from mathematics, there would be no plus without a horizontal minus line. From this we can conclude that blessings never just happen randomly. In order for the sources of blessing to burst open, pressure is needed. That is what is written in the Bible:

As they pass through the Valley of Baca, They make it a spring; The rain also covers it with pools.

Psalm 84:6

What exactly is the "valley of tears?" It is the things we do not want and the situations we try to avoid with all our strength. It is the time when we give up. However, we often cannot imagine that sources of happiness, joy, and inspiration will open before us in this valley. God allows all minuses in our lives so we can, with right reactions, turn them into pluses. What exactly is a right reaction? When pressure comes, instead of complaining, we should begin to thank God that everything will work out because after all He is Almighty God. By this kind of reaction, we turn the minus into a plus. If we perceive all difficulties like this then we will experience the right results in our lives. This is because in the middle of despair, pain, and disappointment we will find strength in the Lord and open God's blessings for ourselves (see Psalm 84:6-8). It is for this reason at one time I made the decision to never complain at circumstances or people, or in other words at life. Even when I want to complain I keep silent.

Therefore never stop when obstacles rise up against you! Never! If you stop then you will not enjoy the springs that are hidden behind the mountain of your problem. However, when you get to the top of the mountain you will find a plethora of new possibilities and perspectives. Therefore, never give up and do not fall into despair. On the contrary, learn to turn the obstacle into a source of joy and blessing. If you learn to do this then you will certainly have success.

Why does God allow all these life obstacles? Do you know that God specially leads us through all possible obstacles because He wants to instill strength of character and spirit into us? He wants each one of us to become the personality He had planned us to be from the beginning. This is only possible to achieve with the help of problems as, for example, our muscles are developed with the help of weights. Without those weights we cannot even dream about having big strong muscles. By overcoming problems we learn to solve life's difficult tasks and become more confident in our own strength, or in other words we become courageous.

If you desire to become a man of action then you have to also learn to become a man who is dedicated to work. Many people have the mentality that blessings and wealth will come by just resting and doing nothing. However, in reality rest is just a break in between your work. Rest is only necessary when you are tired of working. So get rid of the lazy person mentality, because, "The soul of a lazy man desires, and has nothing; but the soul of the diligent shall be made rich" (Proverbs 13:4).

If God has said that only diligent, hardworking people that are not lazy will have abundance then that means there is no other way. This is God's principle and it includes both believers and unbelievers. Therefore, if you are a believer and you think that God is obliged to provide everything for you, then you are mistaken. God would bless a hardworking unbeliever quicker than you a believer that does nothing. God honors our obedience to His principles. He loves you and you will go to heaven because you have received Jesus Christ as your Lord and Savior, with this you have fulfilled God's principle that says:

"He who believes in the Son has everlasting life; and he who does not believe the Son shall not see life, but the wrath of God abides on him."

John 3:36

From this principle, you as a Christian will inherit eternal life and will go to heaven and the unbeliever will go to

hell. However, as for life on this earth, the diligent unbeliever will enjoy it because unlike you, he follows God's principle of hard work. Consequently, in order to live well on the earth you definitely have to be diligent. A slack hand becomes poor (see Proverbs 10:4).

You will never become successful by living on handouts. At the same time if you do not work, you are robbing yourself as well as those around you, and apart from this, you will begin to deteriorate as a person.

Many of us refuse to work because of, for example, a low salary. However, I would like to say to you that even if you were offered 50 dollars a month that is much better than not working at all. More blessings are actually hidden in your job than in your salary because it is the hand of the diligent that makes one rich and not a high salary. If you are a diligent person then wealth knows how to find you. The main question is not the salary but how hardworking and diligent you are. You will only become rich when you begin to work despite the salary and despite the problems and difficulties and despite your effectiveness or ineffectiveness. This is what diligence is. It includes long-suffering, the ability to follow through your goals and focus on your calling. Be diligent and then you will be promoted in your sphere of activity. The Word of God promises this.

Do you see a man who excels in his work? He will stand before kings; He will not stand before unknown men.

Proverbs 22:29

The word "excel" in this scripture could be interpreted as focused and diligent. Only the people who are diligent, focused, and dedicated to their work will stand before the king! However, it is very important to state here that diligence will only bring results in the land of your calling. Only by excelling in your work or your calling can you achieve great things. That is why I began this book with the chapter about how to find your calling. This is very important. The wrong place and the wrong calling will only bring you disappointments. It does not matter how diligent you are. However, if you feel like you are in your place then be strong, do not waver in your diligence and then you will stand before kings. That is what God says. We do not have to be worthy before earthly kings but before the King of kings Jesus Christ. And for this you need to lay down your life on the altar. Work hard every day as if it were the only and last day of your life.

What else is needed in order to narrow the gap between a decision made and its accomplishment? If you are a Christian, then everything you do should be done as if unto the Lord, Who sees not only all our deeds but knows all our thoughts. "...Your Father who sees in secret will reward you openly" (Matthew 6:18).

God is a specialist and an expert at rewarding what you do in secret. Therefore, you should also be a specialist in doing things in secret. Be more focused on the things nobody sees and on the things no one thanks you for doing. Be faithful where nobody notices, where nobody expects anything from you. Then God will find thousands of ways to promote you. This will be a reward for you and what you did in secret would become openly known.

I think this also will give you an extra incentive to work hard and be diligent even when your boss does not notice or praise you, and also does not value you the way he should. This is because you are working for the Lord and He sees everything. If you could live like this then you would see even greater results than you could ever imagine.

GOLDEN TRUTHS

- Everything that is happening to us today is only the result of all the decisions that we made yesterday.
- The one who refuses to make a decision in life is the one who allows circumstances and other people to use him for their own advantage.
- The future will bring a breakthrough only to those who today have not only made a decision but who also have begun to instill within themselves certain values and principles.
- The law of getting results says; never leave the place of your decision without taking specific steps directed toward its fulfillment.
- Having made a decision to do something, it is essential to surround yourself with something that will remind you about the decision you have made.
- A documented vision will help you every day to take certain steps toward its fulfillment.
- A combination of both Biblical and scientific knowledge together with spiritual and physical understanding will help you to become the best of the best in the sphere of your activity.
- Never stop attaining goals.
- Everyone without exception has something to learn. Any person no matter what his status or position is in society can become a source of necessary knowledge.
- Every obstacle is a hidden step on the path to promotion.
- A large salary does not make a person rich, it is a diligent hand that does.
- Do everything in life as unto the Lord.

CHAPTER 8

BE UNWAVERING

Praise the Lord! You have made a decision. This is half of the victory. Now the most important thing is to act in accordance with what you have decided. There should be no doubt or wavering at all. God does not like it when we doubt; "but let him ask in faith, with no doubting, for he who doubts is like a wave of the sea driven and tossed by the wind. For let not that man suppose that he will receive anything from the Lord; he is a double-minded man, unstable in all his ways" (James 1:6-8).

What can help us to be unwavering as we go about fulfilling what we have planned?

DO NOT THROW AWAY YOUR CONFIDENCE...

Unbelievers live and do not know what will happen to them the next day. They waver to and fro moving from one teaching to the other and are under the influence of all kinds of problems; such as economical or political. They are constantly in a state of inner turmoil. This of course, hinders them from being unwavering in attaining the goal they have set for themselves. However, believers have a great advantage over unbelievers. They have a confidence. This confidence is in Jesus Christ.

Behold what manner of love the Father has bestowed on us, that we should be called children of God! Therefore the world does not

know us, because it did not know Him. Beloved, now we are children of God; and it has not yet been revealed what we shall be, but we know that when He is revealed, we shall be like Him, for we shall see Him as He is. And everyone who has this hope in Him purifies himself, just as He is pure.

1 John 3:1-3

While some people are debating whether or not there is a heaven or a hell, we know with all certainty, that there will come a moment when we will stand face to face before our Savoir and become just like Him. This is our great hope. It cannot be compared to anything else. To see Jesus and become like Him is so much greater than anything God gives us on this earth. God's blessings, healing, success, acceptance, and riches are only a dessert. They are not the main course. All earthly blessings are nothing compared to the eternal life we will enjoy in Jesus Christ. That is why God warns us not to throw away our confidence even if there are difficulties and tests along our path (see Hebrews 10:35-39). God has prepared a great reward for those who endure, who love Him and are not just religious but really know Him and honor His Word.

But as it is written: "Eye has not seen, nor ear heard, nor have entered into the heart of man the things which God has prepared for those who love Him."

1 Corinthians 2:9

In the gospel of john we can read the words of Jesus:

"In My Father's house are many mansions; if it were not so, I would have told you. I go to prepare a place for you. And if I go and

prepare a place for you, I will come again and receive you to Myself; that where I am, there you may be also."

John 14:2,3

Jesus left this world with only one goal. He went to prepare a place in the house of His Heavenly Father for the chosen, redeemed, and for those who have been washed with His blood. We should not give up our place in the house of our Father; we should not throw away our confidence. Let everything else be taken away from us but under no circumstance should we give our confidence to the world, our friends, or our enemies. We will need patience to do this.

SAVE YOUR SOUL WITH YOUR PATIENCE

For you have need of endurance, so that after you have done the will of God, you may receive the promise...

Hebrews 10:36

"...By your patience possess your souls."

Luke 21:19

Why is God saying to us about patience? Why is this trait of character so necessary for us? Probably all of us at one time in our life had experienced God not immediately answering our prayer. At that time it was patience that helped us endure and not cast our faith away. Our confidence helped us receive what was promised. However, this does not happen to everyone. Many people who did not have patience, turned away from God for the sake of fleeting pleasures that the devil offered them at every step. However, do not forget that the devil comes to steal, kill, and destroy.

When we are abiding in God we do not lose anything, instead we gain something even if at times it looks like the opposite. However, with Lucifer things are totally different. After enticing us with something that looks good on the outside, he will later deprive us of sleep, peace, and life itself. You are probably aware of such sad stories. Therefore patience will save your soul, and whatever happens to you always remember:

"And shall God not avenge His own elect who cry out day and night to Him, though He bears long with them? I tell you that He will avenge them speedily. Nevertheless, when the Son of Man comes, will He really find faith on the earth?"

Luke 18:7,8

Maybe today the Lord is moving slowly to resolve one of your problems, but you need to know He will definitely come and help you. The only question is whether you can wait for Him and stay in faith to the very end. It is written, "Now the just shall live by faith; but if anyone draws back, My soul has no pleasure in him" (Hebrews 10:38).

God is saddened when people fall from faith. This is because He knows that it is so crucial and will cost us greatly. Only faith in God and confidence in Him give us the power to endure and gain the victory. Only faith gives us the opportunity to fulfill God's will for our lives and receive a reward for it later.

There are no impossible and hopeless situations for the children of God! If you know your God, then you will find the way out of any situation.

NOT BY MIGHT AND NOT BY POWER...

Many people in the world give up after the first try, but for us it should not be like this. However, unfortunately even among Christians there is a lot of unbelief. Unlike David who said, "Blessed be the Lord, my strength!" these people do not understand Who the source of their power and strength is. Our strength is God. We should not go into battle with our problems and difficulties in our own strength, knowledge, and with our contacts, and money, but with the Lord of Hosts! As it is written:

'Not by might nor by power, but by My Spirit,' Says the LORD of hosts.

Zechariah 4:6

If you realize this then you will proclaim before any problem, "Lord, You are my strength and my victory! I believe You go before me and therefore I will not quit and in the name of Jesus Christ I uproot all obstacles," then go and resolve every question until you get the necessary result.

If you can rely on the One Who is the Source of everything, the One Who holds the whole universe in the palm of His hands, the One Who created everything seen and unseen, the One Who created the heavens and the earth and Who created everybody, you will not have any problems because the heart of every king is in the hand of God and God has every situation under control. He will not leave you in trouble but He will deliver and exalt you.

YOU NEED TO FIGHT FOR SUCCESS

In order to endure to the end, apart from placing your confidence in God, it is also necessary to be a warrior in the Lord your God. If you do not have a warrior spirit in you then you will never be successful in life. If you are not ready to fight in this life then you are headed for failure. Only a battle leads to victory. Victory is the result of a battle. Ask any successful person if he had to fight. He will tell you thousands of stories about the things he had to go through. Unfortunately, many believers misunderstand what it really means to be a Christian. Very often they think it is okay for people to scorn and humiliate them. At the same time they think that God sees everything and will judge. Yes, God sees everything but He teaches us to fight (see: Psalm 143).

We need to remember our fight is spiritual. Our battle is a fight of faith, will, longsuffering, and persistence. Each one of us has a million opportunities to be disappointed in life and give up. There are also millions of obstacles trying to block our every step. However, we should be like our Heavenly Father, because we were made in His image and likeness. He is the God of the battle and the fight. He is a God of war. The Bible says that Jesus is the Lord of Hosts. What does the "Lord of Hosts" mean? It means Warrior, the Lord of power, a mighty warrior who comes into battle like a giant.

The LORD shall go forth like a mighty man; He shall stir up His zeal like a man of war. He shall cry out, yes, shout aloud; He shall prevail against His enemies.

Isaiah 42:13

Just like our Lord, we should also not be afraid of fights, challenges, and trials. We should be people of battle and war. We should show ourselves strong against our enemies. Our enemies could be an assortment of circumstances and difficulties in our lives. If for example, we begin our own business, then we should start it with great zeal like a giant, with the understanding that we are not just starting the business in order to make money but with the vision and understanding of conquering and dominating the market.

The reason why many believers are not successful in life is because all they do is pray and trust in God. Of course this is correct, but apart from this they do nothing else to propel them to success. David became the successful man we know even today after thousands of years because he trusted in God but at the same time he took action even if this meant going to war.

Blessed be the LORD my Rock, Who trains my hands for war, and my fingers for battle...

Psalm 144:1

Pay attention to the phrase "trains my hands for war" what does this mean? It means that he did not refuse to wage war. David had an army and weapons. In addition to his trust in God he had everything that was needed for war on a physical level. We should also be armed with everything that will help us gain victory in this life. We need to acquire the necessary knowledge, skill, ability, finances, and contacts. As I have already said earlier, we need to study, work, make our relationships with other people better, and do everything to a standard of excellence. Then God, Who sees that we are diligently doing all those things that depend on us, will release His strength and support. However, we will be left with nothing if we are irresponsible and do not do everything we possibly can, and simply think God will help us. It would have been like David saying, "Why do I need weapons? Why do I need an army? God is my strength. He will protect me. This attitude is demonstrative of a lack of understanding. We need to be fully armed and do everything we can. We need to knock on every door, make all necessary calls, hire good lawyers for our company to be in good shape, and always pursue new information, etc. This is also a fight. It is a fight for your success, dream, goals, and plans. God expects us to have this attitude toward life. Yes, we must trust in God but we must also fight for our dreams and success. With-out a battle success is not possible. In order for His people to learn to fight, God left enemies in the Promised Land."

Now these are the nations which the LORD left, that He might test Israel by them, that is, all who had not known any of the wars in Canaan (this was only so that the generations of the children of Israel might be taught to know war, at least those who had not formerly known it), namely, five lords of the Philistines, all the Canaanites, the Sidonians, and the Hivites who dwelt in Mount Lebanon, from Mount Baal Hermon to the entrance of Hamath. And they were left, that He might test Israel by them, to know whether they would obey the commandments of the LORD, which He had commanded their fathers by the hand of Moses. Thus the children of Israel dwelt among the Canaanites, the Hittites, the Amorites, the Perizzites, the Hivites, and the Jebusites. And they took their daughters to be their wives, and gave their daughters to their sons; and they served their gods.

Judges 3:1-6

God specifically placed enemies on this earth so His people would always be reminded that the Kingdom of God is taken by force. Therefore, learn to fight for your dream and calling and defeat the lions and goliaths. Learn to breakthrough obstacles and closed doors. In other words, do everything to secure your victory. As the apostle Paul said:

Do you not know that those who run in a race all run, but one receives the prize? Run in such a way that you may obtain it. And everyone who competes for the prize is temperate in all things. Now

they do it to obtain a perishable crown, but we for an imperishable crown. Therefore I run thus: not with uncertainty. Thus I fight: not as one who beats the air. But I discipline my body and bring it into subjection, lest, when I have preached to others, I myself should become disqualified.

1 Corinthians 9:24-27

RUN TO RECEIVE

Pay attention to the words of the apostle that says everyone runs but not everyone will receive a reward. People that reach their goals, run in order to receive everything. They give themselves fully and let go of everything that does not bring profit or might keep them from the blessing. They do not just run. They crave to win. God Himself rewards such people.

Blessed are those who hunger and thirst for righteousness, For they shall be filled.

Matthew 5:6

How much do you crave to fulfill God's will? Without this craving, God is not obliged to carry out anything in your life. However, if you have a strong desire, God will not pass you by. He is drawn to such people. Begin to fight until God begins to reveal His glory in you and through you.

When you totally give yourself and strive and thirst, it attracts success. A reward will be given to those who give out much more than those who also run, but do not give themselves to it one hundred percent.

Your sacrifice, output, and thirst will determine the scale of what you receive in return. Nobody ever wins a race by just standing still. Until you begin to fight and work you will be like a sportsman who wants to win but just stands still.

Therefore, just like Paul, in order to be successful you have to make your flesh and your sinful desires your slave. Then with all your heart you have to crave for victory and do everything you can to win, and God Himself will reward you.

GOLDEN TRUTHS

- Only faith in God and trust in Him give us the strength to endure and obtain victory.

- There are no impossible and hopeless situations for the children of God!

- If you do not have a warrior spirit, you will never be successful in life.

- Victory is the result of a battle.

- We need to remember that our fight is spiritual. Our battle is a fight of faith, will, longsuffering, and persistence.

CHAPTER 9

QUENCHING THE ARROWS OF THE EVIL ONE

We have discovered that we all have a purpose! All of us have our own destiny from God! There is a Promised Land for each of us. However, in this land there are also the agents of sin and lawlessness who do not want of the children of God to inherit the land. They will do anything they can to disarm us. Therefore, success will not just happen. It is a constant battle and resistance not only against yourself, your weaknesses and faults, but also against all the devices of the enemy.

When you have a calling from God, the devil will attack you on all sides. There will be psychological, physical, and legal attacks. In other words, there will be attacks on all fronts. Therefore, you need to build protection around the work the Lord has placed in your trust. When necessary this could be spiritual or physical (remember that David did not only pray, he also fought,) because the darkness will always resist the light. Evil will always fight against good. However, good has to stand its ground otherwise darkness will cover the whole earth.

THOSE WHO ENDURE TO THE END WILL BE SAVED

To win a battle you must thoroughly know your enemy and his warfare tactics. To be well informed means to be well armed.

The first way the devil attacks the believer is through him compromising with the world. This is a serious weapon and has defeated many believers that were trying to be friendly with the world. They want to live according to God's principles but when challenged by pressure they do not stand their ground. Then God's truth cannot save them anymore. This is because it is written: "But he who endures to the end shall be saved" (Matthew 24:13).

The devil knows that if we do not endure, and if we divert even just a little from God's standards, then he can have power over us and we would not see the fulfillment of God's Word in our lives. Therefore with all our strength we need to keep alert. For example, the devil might whisper to us "You have given your tithe so many times, where is your blessing?" We now have two possibilities: we could agree with our flesh and with what the devil is saying or we could continue to sow into the Kingdom of God, no matter what it looks like. If we do not give in then sooner or later all of God's promises will be fulfilled. This is because God's Word works. A believer can easily be the head and not the tail. He can be the very best in any sphere of activity. This is all because of God's wisdom. It all depends on whether we will follow God's truths or not and whether we will hold on to these truths to the end or not. If we hold on then God's Word will become salvation for us. Only when we stand for the truth and fight with it, does God come and confirm His Word personally. Therefore, do not compromise with the world. When the circumstances close in around us, we must look up. God will be there.

WHAT ARE THESE PITIFUL JEWS DOING?

What other traps does the devil set before us on the path to the fulfillment of our calling from God? Let us look at the example of Nehemiah:

But it so happened, when Sanballat heard that we were rebuilding the wall, that he was furious and very indignant, and mocked the Jews. And he spoke before his brethren and the army of Samaria, and said, "What are these feeble Jews doing? Will they fortify themselves? Will they offer sacrifices? Will they complete it in a day? Will they revive the stones from the heaps of rubbish — stones that are burned?" Now Tobiah the Ammonite was beside him, and he said, "Whatever they build, if even a fox goes up on it, he will break down their stone wall." Hear, O our God, for we are despised; turn their reproach on their own heads, and give them as plunder to a land of captivity! Do not cover their iniquity, and do not let their sin be blotted out from before You; for they have provoked You to anger before the builders.

Nehemiah 4:1-5

One of the psychological traps of the devil is humiliation and hatred. Let us once again carefully read the second verse: "...And he spoke before his brethren and the army of Samaria, and said, "What are these feeble Jews doing?"

Or in other words, today we would say, "Who do you think you are?" Are you familiar with this? Remember that the people the devil uses against you will always treat you with disdain. This is a tactic of the devil. God never humiliates people. Therefore, if someone is pouring scorn on you and humiliating you, do not be dismayed. This story shows us that those who have been scorned will be used by God to shame this world.

But God has chosen the foolish things of the world to put to shame the wise, and God has chosen the weak things of the world to put to shame the things which are mighty.

1 Corinthians 1:27

If you are despised, then know this makes you God's candidate to defeat the strong people of the world and put the wise to shame. Such is God's logic. It is different from human logic. However, if you trust God and endure to the end, then you will see God's logic in action. When you are attacked, do not cry or weep. But even if you do weep then weep only before God; never in front of your enemies. Then the Lord Whom you pray to in secret will see your tears and will reward you openly. He will lift up your head and exalt you. He will defeat your enemies. This is exactly what happened in the life of Nehemiah. It is a clear example of the type of weapon to use in similar circumstances. Fasting and praying are the main weapons against psychological attacks. Observe how Nehemiah used these weapons when he was a prisoner and found out that his fellow people were in a loathsome situation:

And they said to me, "The survivors who are left from the captivity in the province are there in great distress and reproach. The wall of Jerusalem is also broken down, and its gates are burned with fire."

Nehemiah 1:3

Nehemiah was a patriot of his motherland, but because he was in captivity he could not readily help his people. He was in a seemingly hopeless situation. However, he knew that God was in heaven. He knew the God of Abraham, Isaac, and Jacob and therefore, although his body was in captivity, his spirit was free and he could call out to God. That is what he did and then God did a miracle. The king himself saw the hidden sadness of the heart of his servant and he asked him the reason for it. He asked him the reason for his sadness even though Nehemiah had concealed his feelings and had never said a word about his situation. This was really supernatural. The king was not only interested in what was happening, he also helped Nehemiah.

Furthermore I said to the king, "If it pleases the king, let letters be given to me for the governors of the region beyond the River, that they must permit me to pass through till I come to Judah, and a letter to Asaph the keeper of the king's forest, that he must give me timber to make beams for the gates of the citadel which pertains to the temple, for the city wall, and for the house that I will occupy." And the king granted them to me according to the good hand of my God upon me.

Nehemiah 2:7,8

Nehemiah made the right decision by turning to God in prayer. We also need to run to God in difficult times. This is because "...The effective, fervent prayer of a righteous man avails much" (James 5:16).

THE FERVENT PRAYER

OF A RIGHTEOUS MAN AVAILS MUCH

We sometimes do not realize that a believer and a church can have power. The church can stop the devil at any time. However, for this to happen, it is necessary for the church to pray to God diligently. This is what saved Peter from death at one time.

Peter was therefore kept in prison, but constant prayer was offered to God for him by the church.

Now behold, an angel of the Lord stood by him, and a light shone in the prison; and he struck Peter on the side and raised him up, saying, "Arise quickly!" And his chains fell off his hands.

And when Peter had come to himself, he said, "Now I know for certain that the Lord has sent His angel, and has delivered me from the hand of Herod and from all the expectation of the Jewish people."

Acts 12:5,7,11

Through the prayers of the church, God was able to do something that we would simply call impossible. He brought Peter out of prison despite the prison doors and the guards. However, a few lines earlier we read how James was put to death by the sword of Herod.

Now about that time Herod the king stretched out his hand to harass some from the church. Then he killed James the brother of John with the sword.

Acts 12:1,2

Why did they kill James and not Peter? There is no record in the Bible that the church prayed for James when he was arrested. However, when the same church, in the same city at the same time, began to pray for Peter, the hands of God were released and Peter was freed from the same Herod who killed James.

From this story we can draw only one conclusion: when the church is silent and does nothing, when it does not use its spiritual authority then the devil flourishes. If the church had prayed for James just like it had prayed for Peter then James would not have died. Remember that there is power in prayer! When we as a church pray, we determine the history and destiny of our people and the whole earth. What will happen to the future generations depends on how we as a church will pray to God. However, this does not mean only the church but also every believer individually. Remember Elijah, it is written that he was a man just like us. What did this man do? He prayed so fervently that God had no choice but to answer.

And Elijah the Tishbite, of the inhabitants of Gilead, said to Ahab, "As the LORD God of Israel lives, before whom I stand, there shall not be dew nor rain these years, except at my word."

1 Kings 17:1

The prayer of only one man not only brought a drought but also got rid of it from the earth. As a saint, there is great power in your prayers. The Bible says:

...The effective, fervent prayer of a righteous man avails much.

James 5:16

In the beginning it was Nehemiah's prayers alone that were answered by God and God restored the walls of Jerusalem.

If you have been in a difficult situation for a long time it is because either you did not pray enough, or you did not pray at all. God is not a deaf God! He is not a God Who sleeps. He does not even snooze! He just wants you to really seek His face as Nehemiah did with all His heart (see Jeremiah 29:13).

Nehemiah with tears called out to the Lord not in order to demonstrate his emotions or to show how hopeless the situation was. No! He had already found the way out. He knew that until he began to seek God with all his heart and turn his attention to heaven he would not see the reality of the answer to the problem.

I will lift up my eyes to the hills — From whence comes my help? My help comes from the LORD, Who made heaven and earth.

Psalm 121:1,2

It is important for us to know and understand from which mountain our help comes.

...AND WE SET A WATCH AGAINST THEM...

So the first thing we need to do in order to stand against the schemes of the devil is to fervently and continually pray. The second important condition necessary for victory is to be alert and protect ourselves both on a spiritual and physical level. This is exactly what Nehemiah did.

Nevertheless we made our prayer to our God, and because of them we set a watch against them day and night.

Nehemiah 4:9

What did the Israelites do with Nehemiah as their leader? They prayed and set a watch.

Once somebody asked me this question, "Why do you have bodyguards? Can't God protect you?" I replied, "God does His work and I do mine." In the Word, the Lord teaches us to be sensible and wise. Yes, the devil stands behind every attack and in the spiritual realm we resist him in prayer. However, in the physical realm, in his war against us, the devil uses people who are not obedient to God. Therefore, the Lord warns us:

"...But beware of men, for they will deliver you up to councils and scourge you in their synagogues."

Matthew 10:17

Now I urge you, brethren, note those who cause divisions and offenses, contrary to the doctrine which you learned, and avoid them.

Romans 16:17

Even Jesus Himself said that until His time came His enemies could not touch Him.

Therefore they sought again to seize Him, but He escaped out of their hand.

John 10:39

You need to read the Bible very carefully. Of course, there are situations when God comes to help supernaturally. However, in most circumstances you just need to show wisdom and not provoke or tempt your enemies.

However, we must always remember that our real enemies are not the people attacking us; they are only flesh and blood. There is an unclean spirit that is standing behind them. That is why Jesus said, "Love your enemies..." He knew in the beginning that God made everyone good, but the devil perverted man. Therefore no matter what, we need to be kind to people. We must remember that if God would come into their lives, they would also become good. Therefore, love people and pray for them, forgive them and bless them, even if this is hard to do. Then God who sees our good heart will stand up for us. However, if we take it upon ourselves to judge and return evil for evil, then we will never win because God will not support us in this. Only good and love can defeat evil.

...IT IS REPORTED AMONG THE NATIONS

When the devil does not succeed in turning you away from God and His word, and if he does not succeed in destroying you physically through humiliations and hatred to turn you away from your calling, then he will use other methods to stop you. Let us look at another example of how the devil tried to get Nehemiah off the right path.

In it was written: It is reported among the nations, and Geshem says, that you and the Jews plan to rebel; therefore, according to these rumors, you are rebuilding the wall, that you may be their king.

Nehemiah 6:6

The devil also uses gossip and rumors as a tactic. People who do not understand what we are doing sometimes begin to spread all sorts of lies about us. How do you deal with storytellers and gossips? How do you react to a lie?

Every time that someone slanders us, we can either get involved in all the strife with the offenders or we can ignore them. Then with even greater zeal, we can continue to move forward. Do not waste any time trying to deal with slanderers. All this opposition that the devil is using has been sent to us in order to distract us from the work we are doing. Therefore, it is necessary for us to have wisdom and at the same time to become even more zealous in our work. We should increase the intensity of the work in the necessary direction and maximize our focus on the goal. Let our enemies say what they want. That is their problem. We are not responsible for their words and actions! We are only accountable for our own behavior before God. We must allow God to deal with our enemies. He knows how to deal with them.

Sometimes it is not only our opponents but also our brothers and sisters that can become weapons of the devil against us. The devil tries to destroy

God's contacts and separate us from our friends in order to get us off our calling and put us on the wrong path.

A perverse man sows strife, And a whisperer separates the best of friends. A violent man entices his neighbor, And leads him in a way that is not good.

Proverbs 16:28,29

More often than not our friends do not realize that Satan is using them. Remember Peter who tried to talk Jesus out of going to the cross? Even through good people, thoughts, desires, and projects the devil can put us on the wrong track. Therefore, it is simply necessary that we ask God for help to be able to discern from which spirit the suggestion came. God gave Nehemiah such wisdom and therefore he could refuse an offer that looked good and profitable at first glance.

...That Sanballat and Geshem sent to me, saying, "Come, let us meet together among the villages in the plain of Ono." But they thought to do me harm.

Nehemiah 6:2

The spirit of Nehemiah discerned that this offer from these influential Sanballat and Geshem was in actual fact not directed to help him. On the contrary, it was designed to stop him. May God also give us, like Nehemiah, accuracy in the spirit so that we can discern when God is moving and when it is just the flesh, and also the ability to end those relationships that are not from God. In order to have success it is essential to learn to fight against the attempt of the devil, who through unhealthy relationships, try to destroy us and hinder us from fulfilling God's calling for our lives, and therefore keep us unfocused on this purpose. We must not allow evil and deceptive friends or even true friends to stop or hinder our mission. We must be certain that we are doing God's work and then continue to work and say to the devil and ourselves as Nehemiah said, "I am doing a great work." These words are one of the keys to victory. It is very important for us to understand that we are doing a great and important work.

I AM DOING A GREAT WORK

So I sent messengers to them, saying, "I am doing a great work, so that I cannot come down. Why should the work cease while I leave it and go down to you?"

Nehemiah 6:3

Pay attention to the word "go down." This means to "come off the path or come off the tracks." Nehemiah could not allow himself to be distracted from God's work because he clearly understood it was of utmost importance. It was a great work. We, like Nehemiah, cannot allow ourselves to come off the tracks because God has entrusted to each of us our own 'great' work. We simply must not stop. As Nehemiah said, "...Why should the work cease while I leave it and go down to you?"

Look at your situation as Nehemiah looked at his. Do not think if you stop, nothing terrible will happen. No. It will affect absolutely everything and everybody. You and your work are very important. Therefore, be focused on it, and do not react to criticism and flattery that might stop you on the path of your calling.

Sometimes we stray from the path of our calling because we do not value the calling that we have been given. Always remember that every work we do on any level is important work. Whether we are a student today or a cleaner or a truck driver, it is all very important. Therefore, be completely focused and dedicated to it. We should not be in a hurry to move on until we have completed and finished every stage we are on in our life. This does not mean we do nothing else or we stop developing ourselves in other areas. It means to be completely focused on the work we are doing today. We must place a great value on ourselves and our calling. When unavoidable difficulties and trials come, we must be steadfast in not giving up our path for an easier one. Apostle Paul understood he was doing something great and therefore, he did not exchange this path for some other one.

When he had come to us, he took Paul's belt, bound his own hands and feet, and said, "Thus says the Holy Spirit, 'So shall the Jews at Jerusalem bind the man who owns this belt, and deliver him into the hands of the Gentiles'." Now when we heard these things, both we and those from that place pleaded with him not to go up to Jerusalem. Then Paul answered, "What do you mean by weeping and breaking my heart? For I am ready not only to be bound, but also to die at Jerusalem for the name of the Lord Jesus."

Acts 21:11-13

Paul was ready to do anything, even die for Christ because he knew it was his calling and the name of Jesus was his fate.

Jesus also regarded His mission as something great. He treasured the calling that was given to Him even if it meant He would have to die on the cross. He followed His path to the very end and achieved the final victory over death itself. Then He was raised to the right hand of the Father.

Therefore, the devil will use all possible means to get us to turn away from God and our purpose. May God protect us so that we do come off the path of righteousness, purity, and truth neither in our personal lives nor in our ministry and calling in the name of Jesus Christ!

GOLDEN TRUTHS

- Only when we stand in the truth and fight with it, can God Himself come and begin to confirm His Word.
- If you are despised, then know that this makes you God's candidate to defeat the strong people of this world and put the wise to shame.
- Praying and fasting are the main weapons against the psychological attacks of the devil.
- The prayer of the church determines the history and the fate of its people as well as the whole earth.
- The prayer of a righteous man avails much.
- Love your enemies.
- Do not waste time trying to deal with your enemies.
- Any work that you are doing at present is a great work.

CHAPTER 10

THE ABILITY TO ORGANIZE YOUR BUSINESS OR MINISTRY

In previous chapters we have mentioned how to become organized in order to achieve success. However, without a team, this is practically impossible. Therefore, as I come to the end of this book I want to conclude with the topic of how to organize the people around you and how to create a team of like-minded thinkers.

After you have received revelation and have understanding of what you are called to do, the second thing you need to understand is that one person is not enough to win the battle. What does this mean? This means first of all, that there are people you need who can help you develop and materialize your potential. You cannot become successful all by yourself. You will only become disappointed in life, fall into depression and start to hate the whole world if you are alone. It is very easy to fall into this if you are by yourself.

Therefore, you need to understand a very important law that says life and calling are founded on relationships. These relationships can be divided into three different types.

ONE MAN CANNOT WIN THE BATTLE

Whoever you are called to be, the first type of relationship you need is either with people or educational institutes which have the information or skills that you are searching for. In other words, these are relationships with those who have something you need. They are relationships with teachers and instructors.

The second kind of relationship is when you have something to offer others. For example, if I am called to be a preacher and I am studying in a theological seminary then I have already developed the first type of relationship. However, if I do not preach to anyone, I will not be successful. Even before you finish your studies you need to offer your talents and abilities to those around you. This is how you develop the second type of relationship. After receiving the knowledge related to your calling you need to pass it on to others: to those who are connected to your vision and calling. If you do nothing to improve this second type of relationship then you obviously will not fulfill your calling. Apart from this, whatever you receive you need to give away. Life was made like this: whoever receives something is obliged to give something away. This is the second type of relationship.

When you have received the necessary knowledge and ability and someone from your circle of acquaintances has benefited from it, then a time will come when you are ready to give out even more and to a greater number of people. At this moment you must begin to develop the third type of relationship. It is the search for a larger group of people to serve. Johann Wolfgang von Goethe said, "Knowing is not enough; we must apply." That is the purpose of advertisements. For example, if you are a good doctor but you do not advertise your services then you will not reach those who need your help. They will simply not know that you are the answer to their problem. You have to seek your potential clients and people who need your services, products, and gifts. This will assist you in becoming successful in life and help you to fully develop and use your gifts and talents.

Therefore there are three types of relationships: when you receive, when you give and when you give out much.

The second aspect of 'one man cannot win the battle' is when the third kind of relationship begins to develop well and many people want to use your services. At this point you will begin to sense an urgent need for a team. What exactly is a "team?" It is a group of people who think the same way as you.

It is so true that one man cannot win the battle. However, why is it so necessary to develop these three types of relationships before you create a team? This is very simple. No one will follow an empty head or a man without a vision or influence with no concrete result to show for his work. If you have these three types of relationships then it will be easier for you to convince people of the fact that you are serious and that they can work and grow together with you.

So after you have determined your calling, it is essential to develop these three types of relationships and then create a team of like-minded people. To lead this team, you must develop your leadership potential. Therefore, whoever you want to become, it is crucial for you to be a successful leader. In our church the G-12 system helps with this. If you are already leading at least two other people then you are a leader. Someone once said, "If you learn to lead three people then you will have no problem leading one hundred or two hundred people." How do you learn to lead?

THE IMPORTANCE OF SOUND ADMINISTRATION

Just like it is in the life of an individual or an organization, one of the catalysts of progress is discipline and order.

Order plays a very important role both in business and in ministry. If there is order, discipline, and sound administration then you have a very good chance of achieving a high level of success in your work. That is exactly what the father-in-law of Moses advised Moses to do. Do you remember this story?

And Moses said to his father-in-law, "Because the people come to me to inquire of God. When they have a difficulty, they come to me, and I judge between one and another; and I make known the statutes of God and His laws." So Moses' father-in-law said to him, "The thing that you do is not good. Both you and these people who are with you will surely wear yourselves out. For this thing is too much for you; you are not able to perform it by yourself. Listen now to my voice; I will give you counsel, and God will be with you: Stand before God for the people, so that you may bring the difficulties to God. And you shall teach them the statutes and the laws, and show them the way in which they must walk and the work they must do. Moreover you shall select from all the people able men, such as fear God, men of truth, hating covetousness; and place such over them to be rulers of thousands, rulers of hundreds, rulers of fifties, and rulers of tens. And let them judge the people at all times. Then it will be that every great matter they shall bring to you, but every small matter they themselves shall judge. So it will be easier for you, for they will bear the burden with you. If you do this thing, and God so commands you, then you will be able to endure, and all this people will also go to their place in peace." So Moses heeded the voice of his father-in-law and did all that he had said.

Exodus 18:15-24

What is the father-in-law of Moses teaching here? He is teaching pure administration and organization of people. Without this, you will not achieve success in any type of structure at any time, whether it is a factory, office or church. This is what helps to organize people for effective work in the ministry with a view to achieving maximum results. It is the same as a sweet sounding orchestra. When all the musicians are organized they give out a wonderful sound that is simply heavenly. However, imagine an orchestra that paid no attention to the conductor and played whatever it wanted. Do you think anyone would want to listen to this noise again? Therefore, the organization of the people around you plays a very important role in the fulfillment of your vision. This will account for about forty or sixty percent of your success.

What is necessary for your team to work as a single entity?

THE PURPOSE THAT UNITES

First of all, you should place before the team some kind of general united goal. However, apart from this it is also very important not only to determine the goal but also to convey this to your people. They would then be so saturated with the idea that the task would not only be your goal but would also become theirs. For this you should use the wise advice of Moses' father-in-law:

"...And you shall teach them the statutes and the laws, and show them the way in which they must walk and the work they must do."

Exodus 18:20

In order for your vision to become your team's vision you sometimes have to conduct a lot of training, seminars and develop various teachings. However, it is worth it. It is important that you personally know where you are going and what you are striving for, the principles of success and prosperity. However, you also have to teach your people the same thing so when you are not around, the progress will continue. Therefore, do not think the time and resources you spend on training your workers are in vain. If your people do not go along with you in the same vision and do not fully understand you then you will never be successful.

The second and very important aspect in striving for unity with your co-workers is the ability to definitively communicate to them what you expect from each of them and what their personal role is in the overall vision. There is no point in gathering a large group of people when there are only a few people running with the vision and the rest are just there to make up the numbers. This is the worst thing. I have to constantly fight against this in my church. I want everyone in my office to do specific work and be responsible for something. Therefore, it is necessary that everyone know their place in the structure and their responsibilities beginning from the secretary and ending with the driver and the cleaner. This is exactly what the father-in-law of Moses advised.

"...Moreover you shall select from all the people able men, such as fear God, men of truth, hating covetousness; and place such over them to be rulers of thousands, rulers of hundreds, rulers of fifties, and rulers of tens. And let them judge the people at all times. Then it will be that every great matter they shall bring to you, but every small matter they themselves shall judge. So it will be easier for you, for they will bear the burden with you."

Exodus 18:21,22

The most important principle that we can learn from this passage of Scripture is how we can create departments in a structure and assign people who will be responsible for these departments, and with clarity inform them of the volume and sphere of their duties. This would also include their office hours and break periods, etc. Also you need to ensure your employees understand your task correctly and undertake some kind of test or exam for this. Why is this necessary? The point is that when a teacher or a leader speaks almost no-one fully understands what was said the first time. Everyone perceives only what is understandable to him. That is the reason why we have four gospels. Each one of them has its own details and emphasis. This is because each of the disciples perceived the teachings of Jesus differently. In the end each one of them gave their own version of what happened. For this reason you should always ask a person to tell you again what he heard from you. If he has misunderstood you, you then have an opportunity to convey the message to him again. It is beneficial when you give instruction to a colleague that you record your message on a dictaphone. Later when he comes to report, if there are any problems, you can listen to the message and analyze what was incorrectly done. The system of accountability is inevitable if you want to attain your goal.

ACCOUNTABILITY AND CONTROL

Many Christians, including myself, have in the past thought that such control is bad. We should be able to trust people because Christians always do their work as unto the Lord. However, unfortunately from my own personal experience I am convinced that this attitude to work is not common. It is a very rare case even in the church. It is unusual for people to do what they are told to do the first time without any control or without having to be reminded. Usually the task is completed with only twenty percent effort. This will not do you any good. If you want your business, vision, or ministry to succeed then it is imperative that you check, control, and demand an account from each of your workers at every stage of the work. Never forget to do this. When there is no accountability there will also be no responsibility. Naturally, you will have to develop a system of accountability to avoid the system becoming burdensome for you or your co-workers. However, without this you will go no-where.

If you are a Christian leader and these words make you feel cause you uneasy then I want to say to you that even Jesus demanded an account from His disciples. You can read about this in the Gospels:

Then the apostles gathered to Jesus and told Him all things, both what they had done and what they had taught.

Mark 6:30

We can see here that the disciples came to Jesus to give an account. This is an integral part of working in a team. However, as well as talking about this I want to remind you that apart from demanding an account never forget to give encouragement. If there is only accountability and strict control, then people will just want to run away from you. Do you know that they are always waiting for a word of encouragement, a praise, a warm smile, or a sign of attention from their leader? Therefore, if you are a leader do not forget to encourage your people and smile at them. Do not become weary in doing this. Even if you are in a bad mood, put it aside. You are the leader and so you have no other choice.

Another important thing to know about the organization of a business or ministry is that not only work needs to be organized. Controlling, the fulfillment of the work, and paying the salary is not enough. It will benefit you greatly if you help your workers to become organized not only in their labor but also in their personal and family lives. If you show an interest in your workers beyond their success in the work place to include other spheres of their lives, they will become even more dedicated to the affairs of your company. They will have even greater results than before in your company. Jesus, for example, did not only teach His disciples and demanded an account from them; He was also concerned about them getting enough rest.

And He said to them, "Come aside by yourselves to a deserted place and rest a while." For there were many coming and going, and they did not even have time to eat.

Mark 6:31

One other important factor for the effectiveness of the work of a team is for the leaders to stimulate the professional and personal growth of each of the team members/ workers. If there is no growth on the level of each team member, then they could simply become disinterested at any moment and leave for another structure, business, or church. You as a leader must motivate your people to move forward and continually encourage them in doing that, because if nothing new happens they will only be able to endure the stagnancy for a maximum period of three years. However, it is your main responsibility to motivate people and support them with the fire of the vision so their maximum potential could be utilized in the work of God.

THE HARVEST IS RIPE BUT THE LABORERS ARE FEW

One other thing important for an organization to be effective in its work can be found in the Bible. Look at what is written in the Gospel of Matthew:

But when He saw the multitudes, He was moved with compassion for them, because they were weary and scattered, like sheep having no shepherd. Then He said to His disciples, "The harvest truly is plentiful, but the laborers are few. Therefore pray the Lord of the harvest to send out laborers into His harvest."

Matthew 9:36-38

What is Jesus teaching here? Pay attention to His words, "The harvest truly is plentiful, but the laborers are few." The key word here is "laborers". This means your problem is not the small size of your team, but how much they can really labor and do something concrete and not just dream and philosophize. As you know, Jesus did not have any problems with people. Crowds always followed Him. You might think that having a large staff would be great. However, Jesus with sadness was saying here that among all His followers there were so few initiative, hard work, diligent, and dedicated people.

From this, we can conclude that the main aim of organizing people is to make them laborers. Not just workers but laborers. There are thousands of workers around us. Take any worker and give him a salary and he will sit all day long in the office waiting for his pay check. Possibly my words are too harsh for somebody and cutting him deeply, but it is better to get rid of a worker who is just using the company and not doing much at all.

The main task and purpose of any leader is to find laborers. That is what Jesus desired. You need only laborers. Workers are not needed. I want you to pay attention to the fact that laborers do not just appear automatically. You need to learn how to discover and train them. This can be compared to a jeweler who carefully cuts a beautiful diamond. This is the main goal of a leader, to raise his people up to the level of laborers. That is why in our church we continually hold seminars, conferences, and sermons to help people become successful. Jesus said, that the people were like "...sheep without a shepherd." Who then, if not leaders are to gather the people and make them into who they are supposed to be. Who else should train their hands to war like God taught David? Remember the harvest is plenty but the laborers are few. Laborers are very important both to God and you.

MONEY ANSWERS ALL THINGS

In order for your business or ministry to flourish it is also necessary for you not only manage people but also finances. Even if you are a preacher or a pastor you cannot avoid dealing with questions related to money. This is because "...money answers everything" (Ecclesiastes 10:19).

But the most important thing is not how much money you can make but how correctly you can organize money even before you have it. Otherwise, when money appears you will not know how to control it. Instead, the money will control you. To escape being controlled by money, you should have a financial policy or a budget, or a scheme of organizing your money into priorities and needs. Without this you will simply be surviving. Apostle Paul talked to the Corinthian church about this financial plan:

Now concerning the collection for the saints, as I have given orders to the churches of Galatia, so you must do also: On the first day of the week let each one of you lay something aside, storing up as he may prosper, that there be no collections when I come.

1 Corinthians 16:1,2

Paul challenged them to be organized in their financial planning so that if a need arose, there would be finances available to meet the need.

Usually as the structure develops your priorities change and so you need to be flexible in order to bring changes into your budget and allocate your finances in accordance with your new tasks and goals. For example, in the first years of our church our main priority was to bring as many people as possible to God. For this, fifty percent of our budget was assigned to various evangelical events. We were not concerned about purchasing quality sound equipment for the praise and worship team. With time, our priorities began to change and today our biggest financial priority in our budget is for mission work.

Another thing to know about finances is to never forget to "sow" money. First of all, into the lives of needy people and secondly into the lives of people that have something you do not have. That is the greatest soil to sow into. For example, if you really like the character of a person or the way he does something or his wisdom then sow finances into this person. Bless him and then you will reap what you need. This is because:

Do not be deceived, God is not mocked; for whatever a man sows, that he will also reap. For he who sows to his flesh will of the flesh reap corruption, but he who sows to the Spirit will of the Spirit reap everlasting life.

Galatians 6:7,8

Sow finances, and whenever you have a need, God will give you the opportunity to reap what you had earlier sown. So do not be greedy or egotistical because it is written, "...It is more blessed to give than to receive" (Acts 20:35).

Of course you can choose not to "sow," but if you want to be successful, you have to plan your finances, and the insight shared in this chapter will help you.

GOLDEN TRUTHS

- You cannot become successful all by yourself.
- Life and calling are founded on relationships with other people.
- Just like it is in the life of an individual or an organization, one of the catalysts of progress is discipline and order.
- Do not think the time and resources you spend on training your workers are in vain.
- Where there is no accountability, there will also be no responsibility.
- Apart from demanding accountability, never forget to encourage your people.
- The main goal of organizing people is to make them laborers.
- Even if you are a preacher or a pastor, you will never be able to avoid questions related to money.
- Never forget to "sow" your finances.

CONCLUSION

As we finish this book let us draw some conclusions. The whole world will make way for a man who is focused on his calling and who knows who he is and where he is going. Mountains will melt before such a man, enemies will fall to their knees, and there will be nothing impossible for him. This is what Jesus was talking about when he said all things are possible for any man who believes in his mission, his power, his God, and in God's ability. When God finds a man who knows what he wants and who is focused on his goal and who is ready to pay the price to achieve it, then the sea will part and mountains will crumble and there will be nothing impossible for such a person. We have discovered that Nehemiah and Apostle Paul were like this. Our Lord was also like this, and we can also be like this, if we know where we are going and what we want in life.

Yes, there will be times when the devil will hinder us and we have to give in, but this will be short-lived. He will never be able to stop us completely. If we know where, and what we are heading for, and we are focused on our calling, then we will eventually reach our goal whatever happens. The devil can only stop us temporarily. He may force us to turn back and make some compromise to a certain degree. However, for a focused man who knows where he is going and what his goals are, this situation is just for a time. Remember, there is always a way out for the man who knows what he wants in life and for the man who stays focused.

P.S. Life is given to us only once. How will we use it? God gives each of us the chance to change our life, correct our priorities, and focus on the direction we should go. Let us use this opportunity. Let us stop trying to find reasons why we cannot be the way God wants us to be. Let us stop making excuses why we are not doing what we have been called to do with our lives. Then forgetting the past, we can begin to move for-ward to the prize of our high calling in Jesus Christ.

If you have not yet accepted Jesus Christ as your Lord and Savior, I am inviting you right now to speak to Him in prayer. God will give you true joy, peace and happiness. Only God can answer all your questions, He is the only One who can solve your problems. Live with God, have faith in God - it is true happiness.

God loves you and He is waiting for you. He needs you.

SINNER'S PRAYER

Heavenly Father! I come to You in prayer, confessing all of my sins. I believe Your Word. I believe that You accept everyone who comes to You. Lord, forgive me all my sins, have mercy on me.

I don't want to live this way anymore. I want to belong to You, Jesus! Come into my heart and cleanse me. Be my Savior and my Pastor. Guide me.

I confess You, Jesus Christ as my Lord. I thank You that You hear my prayer and I accept my salvation by faith. I thank You, my Savior, for accepting me just as I am.

Amen.

If you sincerely prayed this prayer, God heard you and forgave you all your sins. Now, God is Your Father, and Jesus is your Friend. Read the Word, live with God and pray.

The Holy Spirit — is the third Personality of the Divine Trinity. He is the One, who the Father sent to be with His children. The Holy Spirit convicts us when we do something wrong, He guides us back to the right path. Very often we grieve Him. When we find ourselves in difficult situations, trying to sort what is right and what is wrong. He helps us by shedding His light on our situation, if we are in tune with Him. The Holy Spirit will teach you, how to distinguish between right and wrong doctrines. He will help you to find a church, where Jesus Christ is exalted.

PRAYER FOR RAPTISM IN THE HOLY SPIRIT

Now, I am born-again. I am a Christian. I am a child of the Almighty God! I am saved! Lord, You said in your Word: "If ye then, being evil, know how to give gifts unto your children: how much more shall your Heavenly Father give the Holy Spirit to them that ask him?" (Luke 11:13). I plead with You, Lord fill me with the Holy Spirit. Holy Spirit rise up in me, when I praise You. I believe that I will speak in an unknown language.

Amen.

CONTACT INFORMATION

The Embassy of the Blessed Kingdom

of God for All Nations

Visit:

www.godembassy.com

www.sundayadelajablog.com

Write to:

mail@godembassy.org

Address:

Izhevska str., 2

Kyiv, Ukraine, 02095

Church office telephone/fax:

+38(044)331 0258

+38(044)331 0259

+38(044)331 0100

TO ORDER BOOKS AND MESSAGES
of Pastor Sunday Adelaja

Visit:

WWW.GOLDENPENPUBLISHING.COM

Write to:

ADMIN@GOLDENPENPUBLISHING.COM

www.ingramcontent.com/pod-product-compliance
Lightning Source LLC
Chambersburg PA
CBHW051805040426
42446CB00007B/520